7 Powerful Ways to Boost Retail Profits

....in any economic climate

The New Rules

A successful, profitable business requires skill, planning & strategy

By
Nancy Georges
The Retail Miss Fix-it

Published by Nancy Georges, The Retail Miss Fix-It @ Magnolia Solutions, in conjunction with Balboa Press, a Division of Hay House.

Balboa Press books may be ordered through booksellers or by contacting:

Balboa Press
A Division of Hay House
1663 Liberty Drive
Bloomington, IN 47403
www.balboapress.com
1-(877) 407-4847

ISBN: 978-1-4525-0343-1 (sc)
ISBN: 978-1-4525-0344-8 (e)

Printed in the United States of America

Balboa Press rev. date: 7/18/2012

This Book is dedicated to

Magda Georges & Robert Georges.
Thank You for your undying support & belief.

I also dedicate this book to all the Retailers
who are hanging in there & striving to make
their business better in these difficult times.

Let's put the MAGIC back in retail!!

7 Powerful Ways to Boost Retail Profits
....in any economic climate

The New Rules
A successful, profitable business requires skill, planning & strategy

Introduction

For any business to evolve, the owner must take a step back and view the business objectively, with new eyes, in order to assess it and make the right decisions for the business' longevity.

I ask that you take a step back when reading this book and ask yourself what you can take away and implement, to drive your business forward in the new world we all operate in today. Acknowledge that nothing is set in stone and that changes may need to be made, some of them big, but that ultimately they are necessary for the business to survive long term.

When reading something and find the thought, "I knew that", pop into your head, ask yourself "Am I *actually doing* that?". We all know a lot, but it is the 'doing' that impacts the business.

This book has been written to inform the reader and make implementation easy.

At the end of each chapter is:

- **Practical Example** – to help illustrate the use of the key tool
- **Takeaway** – key concept of the tool
- **Tip** – to help in implementing the key tool
- **"My To-Do List"** – space to note the things that resonate from that chapter to apply in the business

Retail is **an age-old profession with new-age behaviour!**

Retail is one of the hardest businesses to master. It is constantly changing. Throughout the book, I refer to 'the business' and 'the store', they are interchangeable, a store is a business and must be profitable.

The success formula is impossible to quantify as it is dependant on so many factors:

- location

- customers

- selling skills

- competition

- staff

- product mix

- strategies

- know how

- marketing ability

Today's market place is hard to navigate. Technology has enabled customers to be savvier than ever and demand more from their retail experience.

The internet and subsequent technology has created increased competition for all retailers. This competition is 'borderless' and it is impossible to track all the competition in this modern connected age. Retailers have to be on their toes and ensure that they are adopting best the possible practices so that they can standout and survive in the contemporary marketplace.

Online retailers are included here with 'retailers', even though they have a few operational differences and constraints. They still have to understand the market and connect with it.

Great retail is an art form – it is fun and exciting for customers and profitable and rewarding for the retailer. Some retailers turn their hobby into a business, forgetting that it is exactly that – a business. The financial returns must equal the personal rewards otherwise it is called a hobby. When retail is executed well, it is magic and addictive to the customer. Like any addiction, the customer will have cravings and regularly visit the store.

The current economic climate has meant that retail has changed forever. Consumers have curbed their spending, in fact they feel that excessive consumption is a bad thing. The years of spending and indulgence are over. Consumers will need to be more convinced to spend their money like never before. The move is from mindLESS spending to mindFUL spending.

There is no definitive recipe to success. It's one thing to have the list of ingredients, the skill is in knowing the technique to prepare each ingredient and how to combine them in order to create a masterpiece. This is where the powerful new tools and sound retail practices come into play. The business must create a strategy that takes into account the realistic resources of the business and where it ultimately wants to be and then plot the road it must take to get there.

Many retailers don't focus on profit as much as they should. Cash flow is not profit. A business cannot grow with cash flow. In order for it to grow and survive, it needs money that the business does not need to function day to day.

This book has been written as a tool for independent retailers, although the principles can be applied to all types of retail, who have recognised the change in the market and want to ensure their business' longevity and profitability.

I am not going to bombard you with statistics and doom and gloom. What I want to provide you with are tools that will impact your business in a positive way and give you the successful retail business you want.

We will explore the 7 most important elements of a good retail business, that once established, form a solid foundation for the business to grow.

Throughout the book you will see QR Codes like this (right), read more about them on page 102. I use the Optiscan App, on iPhone & iPad, to read them.

Click on them to see more detail or to quickly link to content online from the book.

At the end of the book, there are links and QR Codes, like the one below, for an Exclusive Access online page for each topic. Each page will contain some information relevant to the topic.

About Nancy

Nancy Georges is a retail strategist, with over 20 years experience, and founder of both Magnolia Solutions and Paper Magnolia. Nancy's career began in retail, as a Grace Bros Management Cadet, then wholesale and manufacturing in Marketing Manager & Product Manager roles for a wide range of retail environments and product categories.

Nancy established Magnolia Solutions in 2008, in response to an increasing demand from retailers for marketing support. She is now working with them on all aspects of their business to increase profitability and give them the lifestyle they seek. Identifying the need for support & resources for independent retailers; she developed programs and strategies that were realistic and achievable, based on her practical experience within the retail industry.

Nancy founded Paper Magnolia in 2004, initially as an importer of high quality products, then developed her own products in response to demand for Australian-designed and manufactured product. Paper Magnolia now trades as an online business after Nancy built the website herself, her first case study!

In 2009, Nancy gave herself the challenge of finding a super low cost solution for Paper Magnolia's online store. "I knew what I wanted as a customer but the journey I embarked on, as a business setting up an online store, was unexpected and not as straight forward as I thought it would be", she shares.

Nancy works with retailers, manufacturers, brands and service providers in every aspect of their business, to create integrated marketing solutions online and offline, that are based on sound retail practices. Her focus is on Customer Service, product, retail principles and retail as a craft. Nancy works with clients beyond the strategy, she provides embedded support as required, She utilises online and offline tools in a wholistic approach.

One of the most versatile tools that Nancy uses is Social Media. She has been using this new media for over 3 years and is now an avid user and contributor in Social Media. The networks built, the connections made and communication generated through Social Media provides clients with tools that were once out of their reach. Nancy recognises the success of Social Media is when it is integrated with online and offline strategies. Working with clients to develop and implement these strategies is the cornerstone of Magnolia Solutions.

In March 2010, Nancy co-founded Social Media Women. They identified the need for a formal networking group that will encourage and assist women to participate more prominently in Social Media. Having recognised the importance of Social Media, the group is a place to connect, to share and to support each other and build a community.

Nancy has partnered with associations, shopping centres and retail groups, covering retail strategies with emphasis on Retail Marketing Tools, online and offline, supporting retailers across Australia.

Nancy's relationships with local and international businesses enable her to draw on a wide variety of experiences and examples when working with her clients to find the best solutions and create profitable outcomes. Her passion for customer service and retail means that she is able to think outside the square.

Nancy's clients value her creative marketing solutions and strategies, that result in increased sales, higher profit, build stronger relationships with customers and provide structure and processes which are essential to their success. She works closely with business owners and staff to ensure that new initiatives are absorbed and implemented by all members of the team. She works with her clients to increase their bottom line by focusing on their store's point of difference, product mix, staff training, media profile, customer relationships and visual presentation.

Education and information are Nancy's main focus. Nancy has created Retail Marketing Seminars and her first book, "7 Powerful Ways to Boost Retail Profits", to inform and support independent retailers and to help them adapt to the new retail climate.

Nancy contributes insightful Retail and Marketing articles to trade magazines and websites that are retail-focused with practical observations, solutions and real-life examples. Nancy enjoys the connections and opportunities that her extensive network brings.

Connect with Nancy, via links at the back of the book.

TABLE OF CONTENTS

Page

 Marketing

I have deliberately started with Marketing as this is the cornerstone of the 7 elements that need to be mastered to increase retail profits and create a great retail business. It is also the one most overlooked by independent retailers and the one they need to learn about the most.

Marketing is hard to define and often misunderstood. Marketing is the activity that is carried out **every minute of every day** in the business to tell your customers who you are, what you have and why they should buy from you.

As a consumer, when you walk into a greatly executed store, you instantly feel good and are compelled to spend time, and money, in the store. You don't break down the individual elements that make the store work but you experience them all at once. Creating this type of retail business should be the objective of every exceptional retailer!

All marketing activities need to be co-ordinated and tell the same story – this may sound like an obvious statement but it is so often done incorrectly. Marketing activities must reflect the tone and branding of the business.

MARKETING STRATEGY

For this reason, a Marketing Strategy (MS) is vital. It sets the direction for the rest of the business. The MS covers;

* The Business Itself
* The Market (including Competition)
* Products & Services
* Target Customer
* Communication
* Sales
* Pricing
* Distribution
* Advertising and Promotion
* Digital (Online)

MARKETING STRATEGY .... cont

Once the business has been broken down and assessed, a strategy for each component is then developed. The MS is a result of Analysing and Planning, must be inline with the business goals and sets the tone of the business.

The Marketing Plan is then developed from the Marketing Strategy. It is the step by step Action Plan that will ensure that the marketing activities meet the company's ultimate goals and objectives. The Marketing Plan should be written down and looked at every day – yes, every day. This is the blueprint for success.

In preparation of the Marketing Strategy, consider:

- **history** – what has happened in the past, what was successful and what was not?

- **customer** – who are they? what do they want? Are they the best type of customer to ensure longevity of the business?

- **store** – physicality – what do you have to work with/

- **communication** – what are you saying about your business? where are you communicating? Is your customer there?

- **product** – is it what the customer wants? is it able to stand against competition?

- **store location** – what is around you that can be utilised for collaboration and promotion?

- **USP** – Unique Selling Proposition, what is yours?

- **competition** – who are they and what are they offering?

- **promotional activity** – what will achieve maximum results?

- **event calendar** – what can you add to the seasonal calendar

- **signage** – what is it saying?

- **visual merchandising** – does it allow the product to sell itself?

- **advertising** – where is the best use of the funds? do you need it?

MARKETING STRATEGY .... cont

In preparation of the Marketing Strategy consider:

* **online presence** – website, blogs, Social Media, online store, collaborations

* **store language** - is everything speaking the same language or is it the united nations?

* **trends** – what are they now? Do you have this element in your business? What is next? How do you identify them?

VALUE PROPOSTION

The purpose of the Value Proposition is to identify an unmet desire of the customer and satisfy it with the products or services of the business.

The **Value Proposition** is the benefit and value the business can offer the customer. Every business should have a Value Proposition that tells their customers and their staff what benefit the customer will receive from buying a product or service from the business that is unique to the business.

In order to create the Value Proposition, analyse the market and define the following:

1. **MARKET**: What is the market? Who is the customer?

2. **OFFER**: What exactly is the business selling – the products and services?

3. **VALUE**: Customer characteristics and desires: what do they value most? What is important to them?

4. **BENEFITS**: What is the benefit of the products and services to the customer?

5. **ALTERNATIVES**: What other options does the customer have to the products and services of the business?

6. **EVIDENCE**: What is the evidence that will validate the Value Proposition?

BRANDING

A **Brand** is the *identity* attached to a business, product or group of products. The customer has a preconceived idea about what the brand is. This idea / perception is created and reinforced through **Branding**. Branding is the trigger and activity to create the connection and awareness of the brand.

Both the Brand and Branding will not be successful if they don't resonate with the customer, therefore is very important to know the customer. By creating the Brand and properly reinforcing it through Branding activity, the customer will easily identify the store and its value proposition.

The store branding is more than the logo and a colour. Branding is the way that the outside world sees the business and must be consistent and relevant. Branding is the umbrella that covers every aspect of the business so careful consideration is needed when it is created.

Once established, the store's branding must be reflected in all elements of the Marketing Strategy and Plan. This will ensure that branding will be reinforced through repetition.

My Branding Notes:

COMMUNICATION

Communication is vital to getting customers in your store and then encouraging them to buy. There are many tools that can be utilised to communicate with customers; staff, promotions, events, newsletters, advertising and online via website, blogs and Social Media.

The best method and combination is determined by the type of business, available resources, time of year and ultimate objectives of the business.

Educate the customer, don't just sell to them, about things such as:

* location
* operating hours
* promotional activity
* why you?
* the Industry
* innovations around products and services
* how to use product
* how to make the best selection

Communication with the customer today centres around engagement rather than broadcasting. They want to know that they are heard and valued by the business and not being 'sold to' and manipulated into buying. **This is the cornerstone of the changes in consumer behaviour.**

CUSTOMER

The customer must be the constant focus, but how many times does a business look at their customer and ask if that is the right one for their business and the long term survival?   Not often enough I would say!

Targeting any activity at the current customer is 6 times cheaper than the cost of acquiring a new one. Too many businesses focus on new customers rather than their current customers.   Whilst new customers are important too, current customers are more important.

Every business has an opportunity to sell their customers more products or services and rectify small issues they may have with the business in order to maximise sales. They know the store, trust the staff and are comfortable giving advice.

I always suggest that clients do a quick Customer Survey in-store – short, sweet and anonymous of course! Offering a small gift to thank them for their time, which is given to them after it is completed, is just good manners and is more likely to encourage them to fill it out, so let it be known when you ask them to fill it out.

The questions will vary, depending on the strength and weaknesses of the business.   Make them a combination of written answers, multiple choice and ratings.

Some suggestions are:

- What products do you feel are missing in our store?

- Which products, currently available in-store, do you feel are not relevant to you?

- How do you rate our customer service?

CUSTOMER .... cont

Suggested questions continued:

* Do you find our customer service consistent from one visit to another?

* Did you know that we offer x service?

* How do you rate us in comparison to other stores in the area?

* Do you visit our website? Often?

* Did you know we have a Facebook page?

* If you have received a newsletter, how would you rate it?

* How do you rate our store ambience?

This is explored in more detail in Chapter 4: Customer & Customer Service on page 54.

The customer wants a conversation with the business owner and staff (notice I didn't say 'the business') it is all about connection. They want to be part of a community and to speak on the store's behalf. A happy customer becomes an advocate for the business and shares with like-minded friends (through Social Media). A connected customer is *an influencer,* with the click of a button they promote the store and recommend it to others who value this person's opinion and act accordingly.

I wrote an article "**Customer Service Is A Lot Like Dating**" , available online at:
www.magnoliasolutions.com.au > Nancy's News & Info > Articles.

PROMOTION

Promotions do not have to be just for a sale or one particular product – they are a great way to shine a spotlight on something unique to the business. For example: a menswear store can offer a 'workshop' or in-store 'demo' on "Dressing For Your Shape". This type of promotion is not just to sell one brand of shirts but will show that the store is a specialist who knows how to help the customer meet their needs and to educate the customer in how to look their best. This will not only establish them as an authority, but will also sell products across the store as the customer realises that they need a wardrobe overhaul!

I am going to share some inside knowledge with you here…although it is true the email newsletters have overtaken letter box drops and mailouts, local businesses are seeing a resurgence in the response to the good old letter box drop! That said, the effectiveness is further increased when there is in-store and online support to the event as well as reinforcing the message via an email newsletter.

The important thing to remember here, is that activity must be across multiple platforms to ensure its effectiveness, online and offline. This is an integrated campaign.

My Notes:

_____

_____

_____

_____

_____

EVENTS

There are obvious seasonal events, such as Mother's & Father's Day, Easter, Christmas and Valentine's Day. There is always a lot of 'noise' at these times, in order to rise above it, events must be unique and relevant to the customer.

Ideally a store should do something monthly, when there is not a seasonal event. In this case, the message is not just "Buy" it should also to be to educate your customer on the store's point of difference, products and services or to show the value of the service and the knowledge in store, eg: cooking event, workshop.

VIP Customer events or events that bring the online community in-store are great for building relationship with the customer as well as providing content for the blog, website and Social Media as well as making sales. Show the customer they are valued and thank them appropriately for their time.

ADVERTISING

Advertising can be a very expensive exercise in order to be effective. In tough times this is not a great use of resources when there are other marketing tools to be used. This said, advertising definitely has its place.

The most effective advertising strategy is dependant on the store, resources, customer and good matching. The local papers and radio and letter box drops used to be the only economical viable advertising independent retailers had at their disposal. Today Social Media and the internet have opened up the options available with very targeted matching that greatly increase the return of advertising spend.

Any advertising should take cues from the topics listed above under communication rather than constantly talking about Sales and Discounts.

GROUP DISCOUNT SITES

The emergence of Group Discount Sites such as Groupon, Jump on It, Spreets, Cudo, buyinvite, Brands Exclusive etc have been touted as great 'marketing tools' to increase consumer awareness and traffic to a business.

They are, in fact, expensive advertising that rely on massive discounting of products and services. They attract customers who are only price-driven, are unlikely to stay with the business and will continually expect discounting. I don't recommend using them as a regular tool, although they can have a place in a marketing strategy.

Think if what you can do with $120 000.00, it is common to see a $330 service reduced to $90 and the average vouchers offered are 500. This is not only lost sales and profit but a bad use of resources.

COMPETITION

It is important not to be obsessed by, but to be aware of, what the competition is doing. I highly recommend doing a Competitor Analysis and research at least twice a year. Investigate:

* who is the best – what makes them the best?
* who is the worst – what makes them the worst?
* what product and services they offer?
* what marketing and promotion they do?
* what are customers saying about them and compare that to what they are saying about the business?
* what are the gaps in their offer?

Gaps in the market and opportunities can be determined from this information.

COMPETITION .... cont

Businesses who copy their competition are transparent and do not have a business with longevity. It shows a massive lack of understanding of what is involved and required to run a successful store and they will find it hard to evolve and adapt when things change. Customers have a knack for uncovering the 'copiers'.

Clearly define the store's Point Of Difference (POD). Make the objective to stand out against competition and to be different,

I have written an article that goes into this in more detail: "**Competition is Not a Dirty Word**" available at www.magnoliasolutions.com.au > Nancy's News & Info > Articles.

ONLINE

Online presence has become vital to the business' success. Currently, consumer online activity is not matched by the majority of retailers' presence and interaction with their customers, especially in Australia. The percentage of retailers with websites in Australia is nearly half the USA figures, 35% of retail stores in Australia vs 52% in USA. This means that only 35% of stores enable current and potential customers to explore their business online.

Only 13% of Australian retailers are considering a website in the next 12 months. Worldwide, this figure is 45%. Only 33% websites have an online store – this is a massive under utilisation and a great opportunity for retailers with websites and online shopping carts.

Blogs and Social Media are also powerful tools business owners can use to reach a larger audience online. The geographical area becomes unimportant – this alone is a great source of increased sales and profit. That said, it requires a change in thinking and procedures of the business so that it can adopt this new activity.

LOCAL COMMUNITY

Are you perceived as a member of your community?

Is yours the first store customers think of when they need your products or service?

The store and the owner should be promoted as local identities. Don't discount your local community in the modern day. Find something that is particular to the local community and ensure you have a product or service that targets this unique feature.

One of the emerging trends is consumers preferring to shop and support their local community. They are valuing the personal connection and recognition that staying local gives them. Calling customers by name, remembering their preferences , personalised service and products are all things that businesses must do now in order to succeed.

Money spent in a locally independently owned store, stays in the community; Of $100 spent in a locally owned book store, $43 stays in the local community. Only $13 of the $100 spent at a nationally or internationally owned book store stays in the local community (source "Economics of Happiness" movie). Local businesses spend locally.

Communicating this to the customer as well as providing personalised service will ensure that business' success with local support.

Start with a target area close to your store and grow the scope to ensure you are within your resources and capabilities. To try and target the world is unrealistic and unachievable.

PROMOTION

Promotions are not discounts and Sales. This seems to be the only promotional activity we see today. Successful promotions are not limited to in-store activity either, they can be run across many platforms, sites and locations. Retailers must combine creativity, flair, sound product knowledge and good relationships with suppliers to create unique events.

Promotions must be consistent and relevant to the store's branding and the message being sent to the customers. In order to be effective and meet objectives, they cannot be a 'one-off'. All promotional activity must be part of a bigger program and an on-going conversation. Otherwise the positive results can be undone if customers perceive it as a 'one-hit-wonder'.

Sales and special offers are part of the promotional calendar but should be used sparingly and not as the only tool to encourage customers to come into the store. The store's goal is for profit – not sales. Encourage customers to buy products all the time and don't train them to buy at a low price or put off purchasing until one of many Sales. Department and discount stores have taught their customers to buy 'on sale', independent retailers cannot and should not compete on this level.

Try to be creative and think outside the square. Don't be limited to what has been done before or what competitors do. Too many retailers are stuck in the sameness of their 'promotional toolkit' – utilise staff for ideas or specialists whose business it is to know how to maximise return and be creative. Again, look outside for inspiration and ideas.

Look at suppliers and their activity. What can be adopted in the Marketing Strategy and activity? Speak to them and find out what works well. You don't need to reinvent the wheel. Look at businesses who are not in the same category and adapt a clever idea to the store.

PROMOTION .... cont

I have constantly found customer VIP events beneficial on so many levels, they;

- build relationship with the customer
- make the customer feel special that they are exclusively at the event
- encourage personalised selling
- are a great opportunity to unveil a new initiative and get targeted feedback
- allow the store to educate customers in an environment that will encourage retention of information over a newsletter or letterbox drop
- enable products to be tested in a controlled private environment
- facilitate sales

Map out a 12 month promotional calendar, putting in all seasonal and known events; Mother's Day, Easter, Christmas etc, as well as one-off events, such as The Olympics. Then focus on 4 months at a time in detail, filling in the gaps with your own events.

My Ideas & Action

COLLABORATION

What other complementary businesses are around the store? Is there an opportunity to partner up with them to create a unique event or reciprocal referrals? One store's customer shops in other stores, finding these stores and building connections will reinforce the customer's confidence in themselves (their decision making skills) and in each business.

This is a great way of building the business's database in a very targeted way and increasing the awareness of the business to a great quality customer. Remember, this collaboration can be executed and / or promoted online and offline.

For example: Gym and Therapeutic Services like Physiotherapy; Shoe store and Accessory store; Homeware Store and Handyman; Book Store and Café; Computer Store and Technical Support.

Reciprocal referrals can work in a number of ways – Let's call them A & B for ease:

- Flyers placed in each business; A in B and B in A

- Vouchers given to customers for the other's business: A's customers receive vouchers for B's product or services and vice-versa

- Targeted complimentary products or services: with every purchase of product Y from A you get product X from B. In this case, the products must be exclusive, have a gift with purchase or a discount that no other customers will receive without meeting the criteria.

- Rewards: buy 10 coffees from A and you will get a 20% off voucher at B's homeware store. In this case, the cost to each business needs to be assessed; A can subsidise the discount to B or A can offer similar to B's customers.

- Joint events, combining A & B's customers to an event in A's store and the next time in B's store

COLLABORATION .... cont

Executed properly, this is a great way to increase the awareness of the store with very good quality customers.

A collaborative promotional event requires careful planning, discussion and boundaries so that objectives are met and the complementary businesses both benefit. This type of promotion can end up being one-sided if not executed well. Seek advice first and then determine what and how to do it. Start small then roll out once experience is gained.

My Ideas & Action

PRACTICAL EXAMPLE

The blueprint for all Marketing activity is the **Marketing Strategy** that incorporates the offline reality with the goals the business wants to achieve.

Brainstorm with your staff & discuss:

* What are the gaps and opportunities in the **market**, that can be filled and used to increase sales?

* Do a SWOT Analysis, what are the STRENGTH, WEAKENSSES, OPPORTUNITIES & THREATS to the **business**

  o promote the Strengths

  o rectify the Weaknesses

  o find a way to exploit and leverage the Opportunities

  o identify ways to eliminate or minimise the Threats

* Take all comments and feedback on board, issues that have been simmering have a way of blowing out of proportion. Staff will often have a solution to a problem as they are at the cold face of the business.

* Develop a Value Proposition that accurately reflects the business now and in the future – this is the message for all communication.

* Who is the customer? Are they viable moving forward? How will the business attract more quality customers?

* Is the store presenting a consistent image?

* What are competitors doing well / badly? This is important to determine the competitive advantage.

* What promotional activity can be carried out to increase store traffic?

PRACTICAL EXAMPLE .... cont

Additional activity includes:

- Every retail business must be online, talking, selling and engaging. Identify what is missing in the store's current profile and start immediately creating the online profiles and pages.

- Engaging & communicating with the customer is vital and must be regular and creative.

- Product review – is the store stocking the right product for with the customer?

- Visual Merchandising & Communicating – is the 'store' speaking the same language as the staff? Is it inline with the branding and positioning of the store?

1. Take all of this information, and other points outlined in this chapter, and write it all down under the appropriate headings.

2. Under each heading determined the store's activity, remember the SWOT analysis and do the same for each point.

3. Create action plans and time frames for each area – they all have to happen in concert with each other.

My Marketing To Do:

MARKETING TAKE AWAY

Marketing the business is necessary in today's market place. Marketing must take place on multiple platforms; online and offline.

Create a Marketing Strategy and stick to it. Don't let day to day events or competitor activity divert the rollout.

MARKETING TIPS

* Do it now.

* Get informed and educated in all aspects of marketing a retail store.

* Be objective and make the necessary changes.

* Implement and tweak, don't wait until everything is perfect.

We work with clients to develop their own Marketing Strategies and develop activities, contact us for more information: info@magnoliasolutions.com.au or phone: +61 2 8003 5585.

My Marketing To Do:

My Marketing To Do:

My Marketing To Do:

2 Systems, Procedures & Policies

Let me define them upfront;

Policies are the rules and regulations of the business. Policies outline expected behaviour and do not allow personal judgment or differing opinions to be the driving force behind behaviour and interaction with customers or other staff. They ensure the tone of the store is followed.

Systems & Procedures are the ordered and systemised recording of actions that act as a guide for everyone in the business. They set the expectations and standardise the behaviour in the business and ensure a consistent experience. They are essential for business of more than one person and ensure efficiency and consistency.

A retail business requires every task and activity in the business to be systemised and procedures created.

Systems, Processes & Policies ensure that everyone acts and is 'marching to the same beat' when they are acting on behalf of the business. Important information can be collected as a result of the team acting as a unit and not individuals. This information can then be used to make decisions.

Systems, Processes & Policies are important, for the following:

* Making decisions based on gut feel AND data collected

* Track and communicate with customers?

* Automate manual tasks

* Identity tasks that can be delegated

* Ensures consistency in the day to day of the business and staff behaviour

Good retailers know their customer, their products and their business. However, in today's market, this is no longer enough. They need to ensure their staff are skilled and knowledgeable when they are not present. Business owners wear every hat; accountant, orderer, trainer, recruiter, planner, staff scheduler, manager etc. There are some things that can be delegated and don't need to be done by them.

WHO DOES WHAT?

Breaking down every task in the business and who does them instantly uncovers who is doing too much or not enough. The owner / manager cannot do every single task in the business, some delegation must happen. It is not cost effective for a high hourly rate owner/manager to do what a lower paid staff member can do.

Invest in staff to maximise the return and profit. Managers should manage and focus on business growth and staff should carry out the roles that are required. Eg: Owner's hourly rate at $50 per hour and staff $19 per hour, this means that the business will get 2.6 hours from a staff member to 1 hour of the manager– so use your time wisely, in managing and growing your business.

Conversely, if the skill base needed in the business does not exist for a one-off task or something that is not part of the regular operations of the business; don't waste a valuable resource that needs to be doing what it does best – outsource to a specialist. What takes a manager 4 hours to grasp @ $200.00, will take a specialist a fraction of the time, and cost.

At the end of the day there are only so many hours per day and a continually growing list of things that need to be done.

COMPANY POLICY

A simple document that states what the company values and expects from staff, incorporating systems and procedures. Every business should have one, regardless of size. It requires the owner to define all areas for themselves and will make them a better communicator and manager as boundaries can be clearly defined.

There is no grey area in a policy, it is a very clear document that clearly outlines what is and is not acceptable to the business. It is the guide and reference to all systems and procedures.

The consideration and thought processes required to create the policies is a great process, in itself, for any business owner as it forces them to consider every aspect of the business; how they want to be regarded by the market and how they want staff to perform.

STORE PROCEEDURES

Every single activity should have a procedure attached to it. Procedures should cover every step from the beginning to the end. They shouldn't be too long or too complicated.

Some procedures that apply to every business are:

- Staff Induction
- Staff manual / Employee Handbook
- Daily To-Do List
- Customer Service
- Customer Special Order
- Stock replenishment
- Order Processing
- Shoplifting
- Damaged stock
- Injury

STORE PROCEEDURES .... cont

Some procedures that apply to every business (cont):

* New product training
* Cash Handling
* Returns
* Visual Merchandising Manual
* Staff Rosters

Policies and procedures should be relayed in induction training so that staff know what is expected from the onset.

POINT OF SALE (POS)

As scary as computers are for some people, they must be part of every retail business in order for it to grow. A good Point Of Sale system allows information to be captured; track sales, customers, products, store traffic, profit and allow the business to be viewed in an analytical way.

Trends can be analysed in all the information captured and used to make the decisions for the business. This data should also be used with 'gut feel' while being based in facts. They also allow remote access to the business; with sales figures, customer traffic data etc. accessible and therefore can be acted on without the owner being in the store.

Ordering & Replenishment

POS systems automate tasks like ordering and replenishment, not only freeing up the owner / manager's time but also ensuring stock is replenished faster and easier and naturally increasing sales.

Remember the system is only as good as the data. A POS system must have the right stock levels and costs inputted as well as staff who use the codes with every sale and maintain the integrity of the data, in order to work properly. Manual checking and common sense are always required.

CUSTOMER DATA

Customer data should be stored electronically as it can then be manipulated and used in different formats. I am constantly surprised by how many retailers still have 'customer cards', or worse, nothing! In the era of email, newsletters, mail merge and electronic communication, storing customer information means that recall and use is efficient and at a low cost.

Collect customer information in-store and online. Don't be afraid to ask for a lot of information and give them the option of not filling everything in. The most important thing is to have at least their first name and email address. Be clear what will be done with their information; they will be sent offers and updates etc. A little incentive to join doesn't go astray either.

This data allows regular communication with customers. A great site for managing customer data and sending email newsletters is Mailchimp. It is free to set up and use and a great way to get into data management and email newsletters. www.mailchimp.com

My Notes:

CUSTOMER RELATIONSHIP MANAGEMENT (CRM)

Many POS systems have Customer Relationship Management (CRM) software built in – thereby automating communicating and making access to information quick and easy. For the CRM to be effective, the right questions must be asked at signup; questions that are relevant to the business and allow targeting only of those customers who match certain requirements.

For example:

- For a fashion retailer, questions about size and favourite colour are relevant, holiday destinations are not.

- Targeting customers who buy size 18 yellow ski boots and promoting Size 18 – 20 ski jackets or defining what products are bought when, and targeting that group at the same time with a special offer.

This will maximise return and minimise time and resources targeting customers who will respond. This will also make customers feel like they are the only person being talked to – this is invaluable in establishing and maintaining a close relationship with them.

In a small store, an expensive CRM is not a wise investment. However, analysing common customer behaviour and targeting them in a timely, organised manner will give the same results as a CRM tool. Be aware of: store traffic, analyse when certain items are bought as well as what other items are purchased with them.

ANALYSE

In every procedure, there should be a step for the recording of relevant information that will later be used and analysed.

All of this data and information is only valuable if it is analysed and utilised in order that future decisions have better success rate: staff scheduling in-line with store traffic, what stock sells at different times of the year, buying more of the right stock, clearing stock by targeting customers' previous buying patterns, which type of events have maximum effect and return and which don't, etc.

PRACTICAL EXAMPLE

A commercial kitchen: the Chef is the highly skilled manager who 'conducts' his staff. He does not cut every ingredient, mix the sauces and wash the dishes. Without him nothing would leave the kitchen, he brings the elements together through good management and procedures.

New Product: Customers often ask for product that is not available. Document these requests in a central notebook (or dare I say it, in a file on the main computer) and review them regularly. If the same items are being asked for repeatedly and are in-line with the store's offering, add them in the next new product addition. You already have customers for them. just don't forget to let them know!

SYSTEMS, PROCEDURES & POLICIES TAKE AWAY

Every store needs them and they should be written with much consideration and care.

Once documented they must be communicated to all staff and management.

Systems and Procedures should be reviewed and updated on a regular basis.

SYSTEMS, PROCEDURES & POLICIES TIPS

- Create the Policies first.

- Write down every job and task in the store & who does them.

- Take each task in the store & write the systemised steps from beginning to end.

- Check each one with team members & refine them all asking for suggestions and ideas to ensure the best systems and processes.

- Re-allocate tasks and jobs to evenly share the workload, if required.

We work with clients to develop their own Systems, Procedures & Policies, contact us for more information: info@magnoliasolutions.com.au or phone: +61 2 8003 5585.

My System, Procedures & Policies To-Do:

My System, Procedures & Policies To-Do:

My System, Procedures & Policies To-Do:

Staff, Training & Leadership

Leadership is a skill and can be learned. Some people are lucky enough to be natural leaders, others must learn the key skills. Please note, the 'boss' is the person who pays the bills, not the leader of the team. The owner of the business is automatically the leader, although they may not be a 'natural' leader.

An effective leader inspires and motivates their team. This is particularly important for an independent retailer. A good leader recognises that their job cannot be done without a team, as clichéd as it is "There is no 'I' in TEAM". The owner is the manager of their business and leads their staff, by guiding them to act like a team / a single unit to achieve the business' goals and objectives. A staff member should not be a leader unless they are a manager, a strong influential staff member can be disruptive and undermine the leader.

Leadership is not effective if they are a "Do as I say, not as I do" Leader. The team should see their manager do what is expected of them. Let's face it; they are employees and not managers in the business, they will do as trained and directed. Lead by example; if the Policy is customer-focused and the procedure is to acknowledge the customer as they walk into the store, and the owner/manager doesn't do this, it will be near impossible to get staff to do it consistently.

Leaders must have authority. They cannot be friends with their staff, nor should they be cold and heartless, it is a fine line. Under no circumstance should staff be Facebook friends with their "boss" or their leader, go night clubbing with them or borrow money from them. Boundaries must be established and maintained.

Learn the skills and acquire the knowledge that is currently missing in the business, especially in leadership skills. This is a very important part of the business and one that must be handled well from the onset.

STAFF

Staff may be the most expensive resource of your business but they are also the most valuable. Resources are limited, ensure the best and the most effective are used. Just as important as the stock is in the store, so are the staff who sell it. Staff are on the front line every day. They are often the first, and only, point of contact for the customer.

Staff should reflect the values of the owner and the business. The customer should experience the same high level of service from everyone they encounter. The owner usually stands out, customers like to speak and be served by the owner, therefore guiding by example is even more important. Great staff give exceptional service. Great staff usually have a great leader.

IDEAL STAFF CHARACTERISTICS

To get the best from staff, they must be given the training / have the skill to:

- have enough power to make a basic customer related decision
- think on their feet
- improvise
- use the right amount of judgment
- follow instructions
- not take things personally in their interactions with customers

My Notes

STAFF SELECTION

Staff selection is crucial. Some people can easily select the right staff, others talk about one failure after another.

There should be a job description for every role in the store. This will be the basis for the way staff are sourced and hired. Write it down and quantify it. Finding the right staff will vary as will individual success rates, but the key is to learn from past mistakes and change what has not worked.

Sourcing staff has changed a lot in the past few years. Traditional 'Positions Vacant' posts don't necessarily yield the best results, with the emergence of online networking and sites such as Linkedin. In fact, some say that resumes will not be required in as little as 3-5 years. Over the years, I have observed that the best staff come through existing staff - their friends or acquaintances, customers - who already know and love the store, or local traffic who see a sign in the window. Now Social Media sites and websites list job vacancies, again using the pool of people already familiar with the store.

Once staff have been found, quickly assess their suitability to the business. Once hired, if they do not meet the expectation then quickly, try and retrain the bad habit out of them or cut them loose. Bad staff and time trying to 'fix' them is a waste of time, money and resources.

Make retention an objective. This will save a lot of money, time and energy!

INDUCTION

An induction program for new staff is a must in every business regardless of size. It must be tailored to the business and continually updated. This not only standardises the training of new staff but also means that time is not wasted with an unstructured 'discussion'. It shows staff they work in a professional business and is something to measure them against, from the start.

Induction programs are beneficial for many reasons, they:

- integrate new staff quickly

- train and inform staff in all aspects of the business

- support new staff, giving them a positive feeling towards the business

- enable any staff member to train new staff members not just the manager

- save time and money

TRAINING

Induction is only the beginning. On-going training program, be it new products, technologies, processes or general refresher, ensures the staff skills and knowledge are kept up to date.

It is important that staff are not only trained in the business and the products but also selling skills that will maximise sales.

Anyone who has trained with me knows I always quote McDonalds, "Do you want fries with that?'. We have all experienced it and let me tell you, they wouldn't be doing it at McDonalds if it didn't work! They have 30% acceptance rate simply by asking this question!

TRAINING.... cont

What are the 'fries' in your store? Are there enough of them and do staff understand how to sell them properly? It is these incremental sales that make each sale more profitable. The cost of selling one item is high, selling the second and third item to the same customers is quicker and cheaper than the first, and therefore, more profitable.

When training staff use all 5 senses, do not do it in a classroom setup every time. Use video, music and / or presentations to enhance the physical experience of the product. Let them use it and become an expert away from the customer. Where possible have at least an A4 sheet with some information on the product so that they can refer to it later. They can put this in their staff training manual.

The benefits of a regular training program include:

* keep staff motivated

* increase expectations of staff and their subsequent performance

* train bad habits out of staff in a structured way without singling them out

* staff learn new skills which increase their confidence and morale

* increase the competitive edge of the business

* lower staff turnover

* team building environment

Product Training

This is a very important part of any staff training and warrants investment by the business. Product Training is not just the technical memorising of the products features. Staff must be trained in how to sell these features to the customer and show them the benefits;

eg. Feature = dishwasher safe. Benefit = saves time, energy and water >> leads to more free time.

A lot of businesses make the mistake of having suppliers provide **all** product training. The owner/ manager / leader should also show how they want staff to sell the item and should impart this knowledge after the supplier has done the technical training of the features.

Product knowledge enhances customer service and in this time when customers are doing their own research, has never been more important. In fact, research shows that most customers know more than the people

My Notes:

....

....

....

....

....

....

....

STAFF MEETINGS

One thing I have always done and found very beneficial is to have regular staff meetings. Sometimes it is difficult to get everyone together in business hours but it is important to find a time to get your staff together. If it is not possible to have everyone together at every meeting, try and organise 2 times / groups that work with people's hours and location. Any more than 2 and it becomes inefficient. We used to have one for the full timers and one for the casuals and it was the staff's responsibility to make it to one of them.

Staff meetings are great for team building and encourage acting and thinking as a unit rather than individuals. They allow the manager to share information one to many, rather than trying to catch each and every single person and tell them the same thing.

Staff Meetings should not be a time to talk AT them but TO them and discuss; the business, updates, what is coming up, ideas and suggestions they may have. Use the meetings to inform and listen to what they have to say.

Regularly, ask them about what customers are asking for and about comments being made about the business. They are in the cold face all day every day and will provide up-to-the minute feedback. It is always interesting to see things from different perspectives. Involve them in the decision making of new products and in-store activities, up to a point of course, as the owner is the final decision maker. This involvement will also add accountability and responsibility. I have found that when staff participate in the selection of a new product or initiative, they are more motivated to put the extra effort in to prove they were right!

Meetings don't always have to be onsite, offsite meetings are more 'exciting' than stand up meetings in-store. They will also work as a morale booster and be a little reward for the staff. If offsite meetings are not possible, find another little 'reward' like a cake, lollies or refreshments. Don't make this the 'norm' so that it is seen as a reward and something to look forward to.

REWARDS

It is vital to build a team relationship with staff in the same way a customer relationship is built. Think of the staff as the business' 'internal customer'. It is important to employ some techniques to further connect them with the business.

An effective team work together like a well-oiled machine. Staff must be trained as a team to act like one. That said, handled properly, rewarding one member for exceptional and above average performance will encourage the others to behave in the same way.

Staff discounts, should be considered as a reward and a privilege. There should be guidelines and criteria of eligibility; they receive it after they have been employed for 3 months, not to be used for anyone other than them etc.

Encourage and reward staff regularly, not necessarily with monetary gifts. A 'Person of the Month' Award goes a long way to building pride in themselves and in the business. 'Sales person of the Month' adds an interesting competition amongst staff that can be very effective – be careful with this though, it only works with certain people and businesses. "Customer Fave" is a good tool to encourage better customer service and feedback.

Tailor the rewards and awards to the business and the staff. Create something unique to the business.

My Notes:

PRACTICAL EXAMPLE

As a wholesaler of a European stationery range, I regularly held staff training, in customers' stores, to ensure that staff were informed about the product and could sell it properly. It was a high price range so training was essential.

One of the products was tissue-lined envelopes.

In training, I shared the origin of tissue-lined envelopes; in times gone by it was important to keep the contents of the envelope secret, especially in times of war. The wax seal was not working as the envelope would be held up to the light and the contents revealed. A tissue-lining was added for privacy and over time came to symbolise wealth, class and quality.

In the training I gave them the information (the tool) to up-sell the customer from a plain envelope to a tissue-lined one. When customers heard the story they valued it more and had a reason to pay more for the envelope.

The fries are the wax seal which features in the little story as well!

Staff often rang me to tell me about a sale they made using the information I gave them in training. Store owners often asked me back to train them after seeing the results with their staff!

At the end of the day it is all about sales and staff must be trained and given the tools to sell well!

STAFF TRAINING & LEADERSHIP TAKE AWAY

Staff are the store's 'internal customers', they need a strong leader to guide them to meet the store's objectives. Training shows them how to achieve the store's objectives in a practical procedural manner. Invest in them and don't be afraid to have high expectations.

STAFF TRAINING & LEADERSHIP TIPS

- Create a profile and job description for each role in the business, this will make it easier to recruit the right person and give them a realistic expectation of their job.

- Train and retrain staff constantly, not just in product but in selling.

- Encourage them to act like a team.

- Reward great behaviour, beyond money, to encourage others to act in the same way, thereby elevating the performance of the team and of the store.

We work with clients with training and procedures to suit their business, contact us for more information: info@magnoliasolutions.com.au or phone: +61 2 8003 5585.

My Staff, Training & Leadership To-Do:

My Staff, Training & Leadership To-Do:

My Staff, Training & Leadership To-Do:

Customers & Customer Service

The Customer is the most important ingredient in the recipe for success for any business – without the customer there is no retail business. Consumers are getting savvier and are far more knowledgeable than ever before. They are more demanding and now have more to choose from, than ever before.

Compare retail now and past, as close as 3 years ago, and it is a very different industry. In the past, customers have accepted bad customer service as the norm and could only buy what was available in front of them, locally. **Today's customer no longer accepts bad customer service, is vocal, sources the best products from around the world and can influence others, on and off line!**

It is my belief that each business does not really sell the products on the shelf, it sells customer service and this is what sets one store apart from the others. I have always viewed Customer Service as problem solving; customers come into the store with a need, sometimes they don't know what it is, and it is the sales person's job to solve the problem or find something that meets their need.

It is not enough to know who customers are, for starters more information is needed:

* what their needs are
* what appeals to them
* where they are
* how to treat them
* how to communicate with them

It is important to also recognise that not everybody that walks into the store is a customer and that the store cannot be all things to all people. So select and define the customer carefully. Also remember: **"YOU ARE NOT YOUR CUSTOMER"**, you don't have to think like them, you don't have to act like them but you DO have to know what they think and how they behave.

The right customer profile will ensure that the right products are bought to be sold to them and the right staff to serve them and communicate effectively, ensuring the store is the perfect environment that meets their needs and resonates with them – relationship is everything.

In the future, the power in retail will be the connection with the customer and tailoring to their needs.

ELEMENTS OF SUCCESS IN CONNECTING WITH THE CUSTOMER

The elements required to achieve success with the Customer:

- Define the customer and their needs

- Then start to build a relationship with them

- Supply the right product based on their preferences in a way that appeals to them

- Connect with them wherever they are, online and offline

- Keep communicating with them

- Show them they are appreciated

By meeting their needs trust will be built and the customer will feel comfortable, they will feel good about shopping in the store, they will recognise the store as an authority and they will trust they are getting value when they shop there.

My Customer Service Gaps:

CUSTOMER SERVICE

Defining Good Customer Service is harder than it sounds. It is not as simple as saying 'please' and 'thank you' and smiling at customers when they enter the store, although these are important too!

Customer Service is having what they want, when they want it. Customer Service encompasses every element and aspect of the business that communicates how the store and the products meet the needs and wants of the customer. It is not enough to build the relationship, there must be something to back it up. Exceptional Customer Service is going that extra step that the customer does not expect or experience with competitors. It must be constant and consistent.

Exceptional Customer Service happens before, during and after the sale.

In the current retail market, the competitive advantage of each retail business will be their customer service, which includes the way they communicate with the customer. It is no longer enough to just have good customer service, every business must aspire to **EXCEPTIONAL CUSTOMER SERVICE** in order to stand out. Despite its importance to the business' success, many retailers still get it wrong and have low standards.

The aim is to ensure customers become addicted to the store's great customer service and come back for more. Each time they come back they reaffirm their decision to come into your store and feel better than the last time. This repeat business is more profitable than the first sale. It costs 6 times more to acquire a new customer versus targeting your current customer. This means the profit is not made on the first sale, it is in repeat sales with happy customers.

To ensure you have a profitable business you need to maintain a high rate of returning/repeat business.

Think of Exceptional Customer Service in the same way as DATING.

I am constantly surprised that service providers think that finding the secret of exceptional customer service is like discovering the Fountain of Youth or calculus! There is no 'secret' or mathematical formula, it is not that complicated. I find comparing customer service to something most people understand helps; Customer Service is a lot like Dating.

The attraction, the getting to know each other/ trust-building and then the familiarity and comfort and lastly wanting to be around each other all the time! See? Just like dating!

Excite & seduce your current, new and potential customers to ensure the relationship is established and grows.

In the past;

* People were looking for a mate to start a family with, a good provider, as per society's norm
* Customer service was not a high priority for retailers or customers. Sales were achieved without too much emphasis on service, because of the limited availability of alternatives, basically the customer had nowhere else to go!

Now the expectations are vastly different;

* People are looking for a partner who satisfies a long list of needs and customers are demanding exceptional customer service.
* Customers value stores with great customer service and reward them with repeat business. Customer Service is now a reason to choose one store over another.

Customers and daters are now looking for 'The Total Package'.

CUSTOMER SERVICE ....cont

Vital Elements of Customer Service

Let's look at the vital elements of customer service vis-à-vis dating:

* To attract the customer at first glance, put the effort into the store's appearance and not just for the first meeting or date, always look your best.

* Be honest, polite and respectful, ALWAYS.

* Ensure you have enough in common, otherwise the objectives will not be met and you will be wasting each others' time.

* Deliver what you promise and don't promise what you can't deliver!

* Be realistic, don't try and turn them into something they are not.

* Use the approach and 'language' that suits the subject, be adaptable.

* Ask questions and LISTEN to the answers.

* Learn all there is to know about them and use this in the communication with them, to make interaction with them relevant.

* Once their current needs are identified, anticipate their future needs.

* Use humour and creativity to build and maintain the relationship.

* When you spend time together focus on them, don't look over their shoulder at what else is happening.

* Constantly communicate and keep up to date with each other, don't lose touch.

CUSTOMER SERVICE ....cont

* Accept constructive criticism as a way of making the relationship stronger and maybe changing some bad habits!

* Thank them every chance you get – show them they are valued.

* Recognise that sometimes you have to lose the battle to win the war.
  There will be times when you have to apologise to a valued customer, even when you know you are right, for the long term on-going relationship.

* Encourage them to introduce you to their friends!

* Surprise them with your thoughtfulness.

* We know that if any of these things are not genuine and maintained, the relationship will not last and you have to do it over and over again, till you get it right!!

The full article "Customer Service Is A Lot Like Dating" is available online at: www.magnoliasolutions.com.au > Nancy's News & Info > Articles

My Customer Service Notes:

EXCEPTIONAL CUSTOMER SERVICE

When Exceptional Customer Service is achieved, the customer will shop without resistance.

This is the aim of any service experience: **LOWER THE BARRIER OF RESISTANCE** to buying. When an additional product is suggested, they will see this as a valuable suggestion that will help them rather than a pushy sales person trying to make money. This is the standard the business must uphold in order to achieve profitable sales and retain valuable customers.

Exceptional Customer Service does not mean dull and boring or overly polite and fake! It means matching the type and level of customer service to the customer and their style. Think of; a Music Store, music playing, individual play units so customers can try before they buy with knowledgeable staff who know Bach from Bjork; in a Junior Fashion Store, music is loud and upbeat, things sparkle and the young serve the young; in an Airline VIP Club Lounge, service and atmosphere is respectful and understated.

PRACTICAL EXAMPLE

I used to manage the Manchester Department at Grace Bros (now Myer).
We had our regular customers, my staff and I made it our business to remember what they had bought and what they liked. If new stock came in that we thought they would like or a pattern they bought was going to be marked-down, we would call them (no email or sms then!) before it was put on the floor or the sale started.

We made them feel important/special and offered them value. Over 50% of these conversations turned into a sale and over 50% of the sales resulted in other items being added to the purchase. We were always the first stop for these customers, which for a small suburban store competing against larger stores, was quite a feat!

RETURNING CUSTOMERS

Statistics tell us that only 60% of satisfied customers will go back to the same store. This means that the aim of any store must be 100% satisfaction to ensure profitable repeat business.

Develop a strategy for potential, new and regular customers. Each type of customer requires different strategies and activities to entice and retain them. Strategies and systems that have been properly developed, automatically result in attracting and retaining customers without effort.

Capture as much information as possible about each customer, for further analysis that will lead to effective offers & communication for each customer type/profile. Every store should run a customer loyalty program or a 'data acquisition strategy', ie, getting more customers' details for the database. Assess customers' needs and develop a program around that. Don't be afraid to ask them what they think of the store and what they would suggest to make it even better. Give them what they want and the relationship with them will be cemented further.

Reward regular customers, more than others, by including them in a 'VIP' group / club. Thank them with exclusive offers, previews and privileges only reserved for them. Don't continually give them discounts and reduced prices. Give them 'value', use this to increase and strengthen the connection to the store.

Keep a track of their purchases in-store, don't issue cards etc, this is just unnecessary admin for the store and there is always the problem of the customer forgetting it or losing it. Record them on computer or on simple cards stores in a box at the register. Once purchases reach a certain dollar amount in a given time frame, thank them with a gift.

My Customer Service Notes:

SAMPLE CUSTOMER SIGN UP FORM:

There are many options and versions out there and the questions depend on the business and the information needed from the customer to connect with them better.

Keep it simple. Try and keep answers to 'Yes', 'No' or a few words.

For this example, it is for a fashion store:

Thank you for taking the time to give us your information. We want to contact you, at the most monthly, and keep you informed of special offers and exclusive opportunities.
When your information is processed you will receive an email with a little gift for you.
We look forward to seeing you soon ☺.

* required information

- Name * ....

- Email address (main one you regularly check) *

  ....

- Address ....

  ....

- Postcode (at least) * ....

- Phone number (relevant mobile or landline)

  ....

SAMPLE CUSTOMER SIGN UP FORM .... cont:

- Do you use:
  ☐ Facebook ☐ Twitter ☐ You Tube ☐ My Space

- Do you shop online? ☐ Yes ☐ No

- Have you been to our website? ☐ Yes ☐ No

- Do you know about our VIP Program? ☐ Yes ☐ No

- Would you like to be added as a VIP to be eligible for future rewards and gifts?
  ☐ Yes Please! ☐ No Thanks

- What size do you wear? _____

- Do you like to buy accessories when you buy an item of clothing or outfit? ☐ Yes ☐ No

- What is your favourite colour? _____

- Does your favourite colour change with seasons?
  ☐ Yes ☐ No

- How important are fashion trends to you?
  ☐ Important ☐ Not Important

- Do you like to shop with your friends? ☐ Yes ☐ No

- Would you be interested in attending a VIP Customer event? ☐ Yes ☐ No

Privacy Statement: Your information will not be shared with third parties.

Don't forget to Join Us on our Facebook Page xxx & on Twitter xxx

CUSTOMER FEEDBACK

Make communication easy for the customer, good and bad. When feedback is received, make sure to respond in a timely, appropriate manner. Good feedback is always easy to hear and respond to. Criticism or complaints are harder but far more important to hear and deal with than good comments. Take the opportunity to hear the complaint and look at the cause, maybe they are highlighting something unknown to the store. Changing this will have affects on other customers too, who may have been having the same experience but did not comment, thereby making the business better in the long run.

Exceptional Customer Service is one aspect that needs to be maintained and innovated continually to ensure customers do not go elsewhere. It is important to ensure that this is ongoing and evolving to maintain interest. Remember, there is a fine line, do not get too familiar so as to make the customer uncomfortable, not too distant or aloof so they think they are not valued or too 'fake' to make it not seem genuine.

This is where Marketing effort, Systems, Staff, Training and Leadership come together, like individual instruments in an orchestra that are okay on their own but make beautiful music together!

My Customer Service Notes:

PRACTICAL EXAMPLE:

Data acquisition strategy: ie: Getting more customers to sign up.

Asking customers for their details is a lot harder today than it used to be. *ALWAYS* have a sign up book or cards at the counter with an explanation of what they will receive. To encourage more customers to share their information, run an offer or competition where eligibility is reliant on them giving their details.

Ask for as much information as you can; address allows the store to post information or target by geographical location, email address allows email contact as well as geolocational targeting, phone numbers allow the store to call with exclusive offers.

If customers are signing up at the counter, they will give as little information as they can. To enter a competition or take up and offer they are required to give all information.

TIP: "Liking" a Facebook business page does not allow for the customers email address or details to be shared, so ensure you encourage them to visit another page on your website or in your store to give the full information.

Product preferences and criteria should also be collected; size, colour preferences, children etc

Remember to reassure customers that their information will only be used to let them know about what is happening in–store and special offers, never passed on to a third party.

The **frequency** of contact should also be communicated; monthly newsletter, season offer etc

Remember to communicate with the customer once they have given their information, there is nothing worse than signing up and never hearing from the store. It leads to a negative judgment being made on the store.

OPPORTUNITY

Currently, in Australia, customers are accustomed to low customer service standards and 'service with attitude'. This is a great opportunity for any business that actually delivers Exceptional Customer Service a reality.

People don't only talk about product good and bad, they also talk about how they were served, good and bad. Any business that can build the conversation around their GREAT CUSTOMER SERVICE will be ahead of the competition.

Look online at any of the Social Media sites, review sites, forums etc to see the conversation that is already happening and good and bad experiences. Comments and experiences of current or past customers sway potential new customers' decisions. Become part of a conversation that is relevant to the business and communicate the strengths of the business. Remember to ensure that this is the reality the customer finds in-store!

CONSUMER BEHAVIOUR TRENDS

Localisation

Another trend in 2011 is 'Localisation'; staying close to home, supporting the local community and knowing your neighbours. The emergence of: grower's markets, local markets, handmade products, home cooking, all point to a customer who is cocooning in tough economic times. Their home becomes their sanctuary and a source of comfort.

There is nothing as satisfying as a sales assistant remembering my name or something I bought before, especially at the 'local shops' as we call them in Australia. When we had the Paper Magnolia retail showroom, we became members of the local community; we knew everyone by name, they knew us by name, we watched the babies grow, walk, talk, we did home deliveries, we shopped locally. Subsequently we became part of the community and the first stop for stationery in our area.

CONSUMER BEHAVIOUR TRENDS .... cont

On Trend

Today's customer wants to see new and updated products and activity in-store. They are more informed and aware than ever before. A skilled retailer turns this information into an opportunity. When speaking with them, show the new product in relation to the core range. Build anticipation and keep them informed of new arrivals, especially the VIP customers.

Consider the need that your customer has to be seen as modern, contemporary and up to date with trends; the "Keeping Up With The Joneses" syndrome. Celebrities, high profile people, new-release movies, popular TV shows, cultural events all create a desire in consumers. Select, merchandise and promote products that will appeal to this behaviour in your store.

Stay up to date by reading the magazines customers are reading, in their category, as a reference. This shows a whole customer, not just a buyer of the item they buy in the store; a customer who buys a pair of shoes from one store may be seen as a shoe-buyer when in fact they are a fashion buyer, this increases the potential of the store to expand their range and add relevant products that appeal to the customer.

This said, make sure the 'WHOLE picture is considered and ensure there is always synergy and cohesion between products, store and customer. It must make sense to the customer in order for them to be comfortable and be 'ready to buy'.

Communication

One of the biggest changes is how customers communicate, personally and with their favourite stores and brands. Social media, the World Wide Web and mobile technology, all impact on not just **how** they communication but **when** they communicate. They share information at the push of a button and on the go. Retailers must understand this and be where the customers are communicating, to be part of the conversation. It is important to spend time investigating and researching the conversation and then, when they are part of it, the store is seen as a leader and an expert voice rather than fumbling along trying to keep up.

CUSTOMERS TAKE AWAY

Customers are driving retail. The reason that retail has changed dramatically over the past few years is not just because of technology; it is because of the way consumers are USING technology and the CHANGE IN THEIR BEHVIOUR.

It is vital to understand everything about them, how to communicate with them, in order to build a relationship with them.

CUSTOMERS TIPS

* Define the customer carefully.

* Watch;
    o what they do
    o how they do it
    o where they do it
    o where they talk about it

* Then tailor the store, online and offline; atmosphere, products, staff, messages and communication to reflect their activity and preference.

* Make **Communication** a priority.

* Make the customer feel important and valued.

We work with clients to develop their own programs as well as an audit and strategy for current activity, contact us for more information:
info@magnoliasolutions.com.au
or phone: +61 2 8003 5585.

My Customer To-Do:

My Customer To-Do:

⑤ Products

I have deliberately left this topic for the 5th powerful tool. Too often retailers focus on Product first, to the detriment of their business. Once the first 4 areas are addressed and defined then Product will be easy to execute. Alternatively, if the product has been developed and designed (rather than simply sourced) the order of the above steps still holds but with the customer of that particular item in mind, it is more complicated, but still carried out in the same order.

Too often I see more than 2 stores that look almost exactly the same within meters of each other or in nearby suburbs. No one succeeds by copying and the customers catch on quickly, so a waste of effort all around and it lessens the effort overall for everyone.

Most retailers founded their store based on a hobby, passion or product segment they thought was lacking in the area. A lot of 'homework' and research must be done before buying or starting a store, especially today.

SOURCING

The Sourcing Model is very important, as it ensures consistent supply of products and new products. It is not sustainable to be sourcing new products from new suppliers for every product release.

We have all been in a new store that we loved because the product was unique only to be disappointed when we went back because it had either not changed, became boring, was totally different rather than an evolution of the store we first liked, or was copied in other stores. These situations show the store had one good idea or supplier and did not plan beyond that. Evolution is very important for every retailer and the product is the cornerstone of the evolution.

SOURCING .... cont

This said, too many retailers look overseas for product and think they are being different because they get their product from France when there is equitable product locally. Sourcing from overseas is time consuming and expensive and should be done as part of a strategy not a total solution.

Do you attend trade fairs regularly? When you go to a trade fair, do you do the research before you go so that you can make the best use of your time at the Fair? Do you make an appointment with the suppliers you really want to investigate further? I hope the answer to all of these is "Yes"!

Take charge of ordering. Make the time and allocate resources to ordering and replenishing stock. I am always speechless every time retailers have said to me "I haven't had time to do the order" –what do they think they will sell? Air?! When a product is in stock the customers can buy it, they will not understand it not being there because 'the rep did not come in'. Yes, I have heard that way too many times. Even better is when the rep has filled out the order and simply needs a signature – that takes a month or never happens. This is simply lost sales and profit. The days of being out of stock and the customer not having alternate sources are gone. If they don't find a store with the same product they will jump on the web.

Automation, through POS system, or similar, and Procedures (Chapter 2) work together to ensure that the ordering is as resource and time efficient as possible. POS systems are the fastest and most efficient way to process sales and reordering of stock as well as providing a snapshot of what's in stock, sales and other data.

SOURCING .... cont

I recommend a Process that involves a review of stock weekly, rotate the responsibility between 2 key staff and the manager. Weekly orders are good for cash flow and very efficient as they are quickly unpacked and easy to process than a monthly order, which is bigger. Orders should be placed whenever an item is **close to** selling out – please note I said 'close to' not sold out. Avoid items being totally out of stock, empty shelves and incomplete ranges. They don't look good to the customer and more importantly they will result in lost sales and profit.

Remember: no stock = no sales!

SUPPLIERS

How often do you communicate with your existing suppliers? What opportunities are available with the people and brands you already know? In the same way it is 6 times cheaper to deal with an existing customer over acquiring a new one (Chapter 4), it is far more efficient to build a relationship with key suppliers. Use the opportunity to make the store important to their business and in turn receive special offers, product and treatment.

Whenever I received a call from a new supplier or a rep who wanted to show me product, 9 times out of 10, I made time to see them. One doesn't know where the next 'idea' or 'hot product' will come from. These people could be a great opportunity, especially new suppliers who will build a relationship with their customers and not forget one of their first.

I read every email I receive from a supplier so that I am up to date and don't miss any opportunities. Reports from email campaigns show retailers are not opening supplier newsletters which is unfortunate for the supplier and even more so for the retailer. This will only get increase as retailers become more savvy and comfortable with technology.

SUPPLIERS .... cont

Like the cost of acquiring new customers, adding new ranges/suppliers draws additional resources; Codes need to be loaded into the system, space needs to be allocated in the store, staff need to be trained, relationships need to be built etc. This is a very time consuming process that is then duplicated for every new range / supplier. For this reason, new key product releases should be 2 – 4 times a year and always around the same time for efficiency.

Don't chop and change suppliers for the sake of it. Have a Product Strategy and carry out a supplier audit. The objective is to have the lowest number of suppliers, as is possible, and buy a good assortment from them. Saving time and money, as mentioned above, as well as ensuring your freight costs are minimised and profit is maximised. More often than not most retailers have over 30 suppliers – this is not sustainable or optimal for a retail store.

It makes sense; when an item is getting low or sold out, there will be a few things that can be ordered from the supplier who supplies a wide range of products, so there is not a problem reaching minimum order values or amortising freight. If that item is the only thing from that supplier putting that one product back in stock is expensive in terms of freight and minimum spend.

A good relationship with suppliers can result in special treatment. Most suppliers have access to more product than they offer for sale. There is a great opportunity for both supplier and retailer here. The supplier buys more volume from their supplier (which opens the discussion for better pricing) and they reduce their overall freight bill. The retailer has access to stock no-one else has in the country or their state, saves a lot of time and money as they don't have to find the manufacturer or figure out the import process and freight, as well as benefiting from better than regular wholesale pricing and reduced freight costs. If the retailer is unable to take delivery of the whole shipment and they have a good relationship with their supplier, chances are that they will be able to store it for little or no cost. I used to share containers and delivery costs with my customers for stock that they would then stock exclusively in their store, and it saved money for both of us.

SUPPLIERS .... cont

When assessing suppliers consider how savvy and up to date they are. Seek suppliers who will enhance your business as well as support you with more than just product;

* staff training

* sales information

* product information

* collateral to use in-store (signage, displays etc)

* assistance with display and promotional ideas

* images for the website

* links to the store site

* promoting the store as a stockist and driving traffic to the store

My Supplier Notes:

PRODUCT MIX

Retailers should be 'shopping' for new products and ideas 24 hours a day, 7 days a week, 52 weeks a year. Not only when they are going to a trade fair or when a sales rep calls. Every retail business must have a Product Cycle and Buying Budget that reflect the sales' ebb and flow throughout the year.

High sale times require more regular ordering and more funds allocated to buying them. Buying Budgets should be calculated based on cash flow, sales & profit and should be strictly adhered to – except for Customer Special Orders, which are a firm sale (and should be paid for upfront before ordering).

The key to the correct mix is dependant on the type of store, competition, customer profile and the stock sold. What does not change is that every retailer should have core product that the customer knows and is stocked all year round. New product is co-ordinated with this core range. The core range should evolve too but this must be subtle.

Product that is sourced interstate or overseas will add an interesting element to the product mix that other stores won't have. This should not be the entire product range but used wisely it is a nice facet. Use this product to show the value of the locally sourced products. Imported product should be more expensive than local product. This is a good selling tool for the mid priced/ higher profit items.

Calculate a percentage to be applied to the product mix - X% existing and Y% new. X should be a larger than Y (in most cases), where Y is the fashion/new component. Existing 'X' can be existing suppliers or products (obviously fashion is a little different as the whole range changes from one season to the next). Then 'Y' is either brand new product or suppliers **that can be co-ordinated with the existing ranges**, thereby making them look new and fresh too.

PRODUCT MIX....cont

Customers like to find 'staples' or basics – there is nothing worse than going to your favourite homeware store and not being able to buy a white pillow case or table cloth. Yes they are not interesting, sexy or eye catching but they are a good basic. A white table cloth works with a wide range of fashion tableware and home furnishings that are easily changed from one season to the next. This is what brings the customer in-store regularly.

Knowing the customer well ensures new products compliment the existing range as well as maximise the opportunity for add-on sales. Think of the customer as a consumer, not just the customer who buys from your store. What else do they buy that co-ordinates with the stock in-store that they cannot currently get in-store? It makes sense to sell more to the current customer and is profitable too!

Your product mix should be made up of products that:

* **catch the eye and draw customers into the store** – these may be sold at less than full margin

* **new products** – some will become staples and some will fall into other categories

* **the 'trend' / fashion items** – these have a short life, quick in, quick out

* **the staples / basics** – tried and tested

* **something unique** – will raise customer's eyebrows

My Product Mix Notes:

PRODUCT MIX....cont

Exclusivity

I continually hear from retailers that they want product exclusively which is often not realistic (this can almost be a topic on its own!). This must be part of the Product Strategy and is dependant on many things, including but not exclusive to:

* the type of business

* the volume that is purchased

* the frequency of purchasing

* the percentage of the total range that is purchased

It makes sense to have different products from the store next door or even in the same shopping street. Demanding that a supplier not sell into an area is futile and shows a lack of understanding. Suppliers need volume to make a product commercially viable and store the levels of stock required to ensure that orders can be shipped directly from a local warehouse. Before making the request, ensure that high enough level of sales are achieved so that exclusivity, for more than the street you operate in, is financially viable to the supplier.

As mentioned above, exclusivity is an option if the retailer is willing to invest in stock and consider a different model. This requires new thinking and processes.

That said, do not look at a product that is available at least on your block if not a few blocks around your store. How does this add value to the store and make it stand out? What will this tell the customer about you and your expertise? If there are no options and an alternate supplier is not available or that options are limited, then the retailer must take a long hard look at their business and make the necessary changes to differentiate themselves.

Be aware of the next trend in your category. Researching trends is important and the time must be made online and offline. Magazines, media and websites are a great start. Subscribe to the relevant newsletters and trade associations – it is their job to be up to date and ahead of the market. A very important part of any retailer's job is to stay informed and educate themselves in the changes, threats and opportunities in their business.

PRODUCT CYCLE

Every store must have an overall Product Cycle that encompasses a Product Life Cycle for each product. An effective Product Cycle will ensure that the product flow is managed based on the activity of the business and will address the **introduction, growth, maturity** and **decline** of a product and the related activity. This cycle can happen very quickly today so retailers must be prepared.

Think of a Product Life Cycle like knowing when to leave a party. If you leave the party at the right time – at the beginning of the 'decline' – the memories and experience will be happy ones. Wait just a little too long and it can be very ugly and complications can arise, wiping out the nice memories and experience.

Keeping a product for too long will give the same results; ugly to look at, lost sales & profitability and bad impression to the customer. There is nothing worse than seeing the same sad old stock on a shelf – or worse – grouped with other sad stock, over and over again. As soon as a product sales start to slow down, the planned activity for the 'decline' stage should be activated.

As a product enters the 'decline' stage – don't slash prices immediately, group it with other items in decline and reduce as a 'pack' or 'kit'. Offer this to VIP customers first (with a time limit attached) and then put it on the floor at this reduce price. After a certain time, as defined by the Product Strategy and the Product Cycle, reduce it further.

Continue to reduce these items until they are cleared. As long as they are sitting there not selling at a price the retailer thinks is 'reasonable', they are taking up space and money that can be used for product that sells well with full margin. The longer the retailer waits, the more the customer will see this stock sitting there and be less inclined to come back. Mistakes are made with the wrong items bought or sudden economic circumstances mean that some things just don't sell. Don't make the mistake of waiting too long. Turn them into cash and buy a more profitable product.

PRODUCT CYCLE .... cont

Being on constant sale is not ideal – even worse is the 'sale' table or the 'sale' corner that detracts from the rest of the store. If cash flow is not an issue then do what department stores used to do and take these items out the back and bring them out twice a year. However, most retailers need to clear their stock and cannot afford to do this. So have a technique of clearing the products subtly and leverage the VIP customer in these cases.

Of course it is best to minimise having a large number of items to clear by buying well and managing the products carefully. It is always best to buy a small quantity of a few items and assess them rather than buy a large quantity of something, because it was a better price or no-one else has it, and be stuck with it.

Product that is not kept in stock by a supplier should only be considered for 'indent' or one-off delivery, if at all. This product has a very short cycle and must be communicated to the customer as a 'limited availability, buy it now" product. By peppering the product mix with these products, customers will consider visiting the store more and learning to buy when they see something as it may not be available the next time they visit. Co-ordinating them with other products will ensure add on sales or up-selling to something similar with better stock availability.

My Product Cycle Notes:

PRACTICAL EXAMPLE

Scenario 1

A pan is **$200.00 RRP** with **$100.00 cost** is reduced to **$170.00**, the retailer still makes a profit of $70.00, there are **10** of them, they have been in-store for **5 months**. New colours are arriving and this is last season's colour and there are no other items in that colour.

- After a week it is still on the floor – now it is costing the retailer money ie. 'rent'
  Sold 1 = $ 170.00 cash $ 70.00 margin

- 2nd week is still costing money – the lost sales of having full priced merchandise on the shelf as well as the lost sale & rent

- 4th week it has to be reduced to $150.00 as new stock is ready to be ordered and the store owner is insisting that new product wont be ordered until old product is gone.
  Sold 2 = $ 300.00 cash $ 100.00 margin

- 6th week, customers have seen the new colours elsewhere and start to comment that they bought it as they couldn't wait any longer
  reduced to $80.00 to clear.
  Sold 4 = $ 320.00 cash LOSS $ 80.00 margin

Overall: 6 WEEKS
they gained $ 890.00 cash + $ 90.00 margin & still have 3 pieces of old stock

PRACTICAL EXAMPLE .... cont

Scenario 2

A pan is **$200.00 RRP** with **$100.00 cost** is reduced to **$150.00**, the retailer still makes a profit of $50.00, there are **10** of them, they have been in-store for **5 months**. New colours are arriving and this is last season's colour and there are no other items in that colour.

- After a week it is still on the floor – now it is costing the retailer money ie.'rent'
  Sold 2 = $ 300.00 cash $ 100.00 margin + **new stock ordered**

- 2nd week is still costing money reduced to $ 130.00
  Sold 3 = $ 390.00 cash $ 90.00 margin
  - **new stock arrives** full priced next to the 5 remaining

- 3rd week reduced to $ 100.00 sold 5 = $ 500.00 cash
  ALL GONE
  + sold 3 full sets of new colours @ $ 850.00 ea = $ 2550.00 (cost price of $ 330.00)

Overall: 3 WEEKS
they gained $ 3 740.00 cash + $ 1750.00 margin & old stock = 0

A skilled retailer will know what does and does not sell. If the store is constantly stuck with slow moving stock or is constantly marking down stock then there is something wrong with the buying skill and the final decision maker and the process. Scenario 1 above shows a retailer who is operating with very dated practices and poor judgment. The retailer in Scenario 2 is able to assess and respond to what is happening in-store and maximise sales and profitability.

PRICING

Too often, retailers get pricing and margin wrong. They only consider the price of an item as the cost in 'Cost Price' and 'Profit' to be 'Sales – Cost'. This is incorrect, 'Sales – Cost = Margin'

PROFIT = Margin – Cost of Goods

Everything a retailer spends money on to sell the products should be calculated in the 'Cost of Goods' (CoG); electricity, rent, staff, paper, equipment, printer toner, bags etc. In calculating margin, annual expenses should be added together and added to the overall cost of goods so that margin covers the CoG and Profit required for the business. If this is not done, then the margin usually only covers the expenses of the business and there is little or no profit.

Freight and the time to expedite orders are added costs that must be built into pricing, especially for product that is sourced interstate or overseas. Often these are a high percentage of the cost price. Another reason to minimise suppliers and maximise the number of products that are purchased from them, as discussed above.

The Product Strategy should include a Pricing Strategy. The retailer must have a thorough knowledge of the costs, expenses and required margin in order to calculate the correct margin needed for a profitable business and then apply this to the products sold in setting the sell price.

Calculating margin should not be approached like an accountant. In this day and age a retail business cannot be run using a standard margin percentage across all products. By having the figures at their disposal, a retailer must set an average margin percentage. They will then use their discretion to set some items above and some below, in-line with the product strategy, as long as the average margin is correct.

For eg: the required margin might be 60% for the business – some items may have 40% margin, fad items and available in a few stores - other items are 80% margin as they are rare and not readily available so can be priced higher – and most items are 60% margin.

PRICING....cont

Often the price is simply bound by the supplier's price and what the market will pay for it. If it is less than the store's required margin but fills a gap in the ranging and will enhance the store's offer then consider stocking it. The important thing to note is that this should only be a small percentage of what the store stocks otherwise profitability will not be achieved. This should be outlined in the Product and Pricing Strategy.

Different types of retail stores will have differing margin requirements. If unsure, discuss with suppliers and look at the marketplace. Every business must define the product mix and margin mix.

By having some items higher than the average required margin and some lower with volume and timing in mind, means that the overall required margin will be achieved. Applying this to the product mix, it could look something like this:

* **Products that catch the eye and draw customers into the store – high margin** as they will need to be marked down after the novelty is worn to clear it quickly, as it cannot be in-store for long.

* **'Trend' / fashion items** – short life, **higher than usual margin** as they will need to be marked down when the trend is over, customers will pay more for these items when they arrive in-store, as they are less price-sensitive for the life of the trend.

* **The staples / basics** – apply **average required margin** to these items, customers will be price-sensitive with these items as they can compare them to like items in other stores.

* **Something unique – highest margin**, customers will pay premium for unique items.

* **Impulse, fast moving & 'entry level' items – low margin**; customers see these items in other stores, so they are not unique to the store; they don't necessarily come into the store with the intention to buy something like that; they are stocked with the sole purpose of an entry price point and the objective to build relationship or 'up-sell' them, as per the strategy. These **products** are better to have than constantly reducing full priced new stock. This group should be a small one in the store and not a growing one.

PRICING....cont

Other considerations in setting the price include:

* Market prices

* Competitor activity

* The stage of the Product Life Cycle

* Economic Climate

* Customer's perception

Low prices are not ideal either and could do harm in the long term to profit and perception, If customers constantly comment about the 'low price' and there is little or no competition, consider removing the product from the shop floor, repricing and replacing it a week later.

It is not an easy or straight forward process by any means and should constantly be refined and monitored. Don't be afraid to review or change prices. Make the necessary changes in order to remain competitive and profitable.

My Pricing Notes:

PRACTICAL EXAMPLE

A GIFT STORE

The assortment and appeal in product is wide in a Gift Store. That said; there are some considerations:

- what price range?
- who are the gifts for?
- what is the theme?

So we are a general gift store with low to mid-priced items and the theme is general interest.

Core Product:

- Gift boxes
- Gift wrap
- Ribbons & cards
- Technology accessories: iPod, iPhone, iPad covers in fashion print or colour
- Magnets – so many themes & ideas
- Green & Fair Trade products – the consumer values these standards
- Products for men, such as cufflinks, pens, clocks, tie-pins
- Quirky slippers
- Lifestyles are changing and people are spending more time at home – add ranges that satisfy this need, like cool lounge music, citronella candles
- Sports, memorabilia and board games, are all products that have a loyal returning customer, look at ranges with new eyes
- Books – core & trend
- Stationery as a gift: Pens, Cards, journals, notecard & writing sets
- Frames – core and fashion
- Pet products, mats, beds, collars toys..
- Animal prints and figurines (group together)
- Quirky items to make your customer smile eg: wind-up insects & motorised dogs
- Contemporary Australiana product if you are in an area attracting tourists
- Toys
- Food in great packaging

Trend / New / Fast Moving Product

* Leveraging a "Hot Right Now" TV Show, ie: Cooking themed products a la Masterchef
* Green & Fair Trade products – the consumer values these standards
* Drink Bottles, printed in great patterns & colours
* Books – trend topics or current celebrities
* Frames – in fashion / trend colours & materials
* Gadgets and things that make them smile
* Different Impulse items at the register

As can be seen above, trend items can be the same as core items but with fashion / trend themes, colours or materials.

Think about what the customer needs for the total purchase – this includes wrap and card as well as the product – don't give them a reason to go elsewhere.

Margin:

* on the core items should be as per the store requirement
* Trend can be above and below requirement based on the market
* Men's Gifts can attract a higher than regular margin as they are not easy to find.

PRODUCTS TAKE AWAY

The best thing to do is think of the product mix, store, staff and collateral as one product. Make this the Unique Selling Proposition. Take the ingredients and make your own dish!

This will ensure it is harder to replicate and copy by the competition.

PRODUCTS TIPS

* Ensure the first 4 steps have been completed.

* Audit the Sourcing Model being used and make necessary changes.

* Audit the current suppliers or

  New businesses: only consider suppliers who carry a good

  assortment of product

  All: Select savvy suppliers who understand how to support

  their customers

* Know what the customer is buying, as well as when and where they are buying similar products.

* Determine the Product Strategy for the store, which encompasses:
  o Product Mix
  o Pricing Strategy
  o Product Life Cycle

* Do the work on margin, profit and pricing - with an accountant if necessary.

We work with clients analyse their current sourcing, selection and selling activity and develop solutions for the business that will suit today's marketplace.
Contact us for more information: info@magnoliasolutions.com.au or phone: +61 2 8003 5585.

My Products To-Do:

My Products To-Do:

6 Visual Communication

So much of what we learn and notice is non-verbal, up to 93% of a first impression comes from non-verbal communication. So it is vital that store visual communication, verbal and non-verbal, tells the story as the branding and strategy want it told.

Visual Communication incorporates, but is not exclusive to, the following elements in the store and in external communication:

* product presentation
* signage
* lighting
* visual merchandising
* staff
* body language
* overall ambiance
* product itself

There must be continuity in all of the communication.

Remember, if 93% of communication is non-verbal and there is an inconsistent element, it will disturb and distort the message being sent, sometimes without the customer actually knowing what it is.

My Visual Communication Notes:

BRANDING

Branding in-store and in all communication is an important visual communicator. Everything the customer sees and experiences in-store and after the sale will impact their perception of the brand.

Once the brand has been established and the branding defined; the colour, font, style and sensibility must be replicated in every aspect in-store, considering the above as well:

* Use the colour of the Brand throughout the store; walls, trims, signs, bags, promotional material

* Use the logo & fonts of the Brand throughout the store; signs, letters, bags, promotional material

* Use the store by-line or 'slogan' in verbal as well as written communication

* Consider a uniform, corporate colour or aprons if appropriate

* Choose music that reflects the Brand values and customer preferences

* The tone and styling of displays should be aligned with the tone and style of the Brand

STORE FRONT

The first point of 'contact' is the front of the store – ensure the store branding, image and offer is reflected here. Can the customer tell who and what the store is at a glance? Does it excite and entice?

Creating amazing, inspiring front windows give customers and passing traffic a snapshot of the business as well as reinforcing that the store is the one with knowledge and authority in its field, as well as makes it a talking point in the local community.

INSIDE THE STORE

Once inside the store, the customer must be excited and inspired. Customers who are drawn by the front of the store, advertising and promotional material, will be expecting the same, if not better, inside. The store should 'speak' to the customer, in their 'language'.

Knowing the customer well, will ensure the ambience and environment, including: visual merchandising, music, service and presentation, are in line with their preferences.

Staff and Customer Service are a large part of the atmosphere inside the store and should not be forgotten.

LIGHTING

Lighting is very important inside the store. When the customer enters the store, they should not be blasted with bright light – but it should not be night club dark either!!

Use lighting to

- Ensure the front window can be seen from outside in daytime and night time

- Direct store traffic

- Highlight key areas from the front door, such as:
    - visual merchandising points
    - new product
    - displays
    - the register

Remember to invest in energy efficient lighting, there are a lot of options available.

FRONT WINDOW

I love nothing better than a clever, interesting, creative, enticing store window. The first time I went to New York & Europe I took hundreds of photos of store windows (that is saying something – this was pre digital cameras!). At the time, Australian retailers were sorely lacking in creating impact in store windows. Happily, now in Australia, independent retailers are increasingly creating wonderful store windows.

Some Tips for a striking and effective store window:

* Front windows should look good from the outside AND the inside! Either cover the back of the window so that the 'ugly' bits are not seen or create a window that is 2-sided.

* As soon as something is sold from the window, fill the gap as soon as possible. As a rule, once a third of the products in the window are sold, change it.

* Props, trims and effects will add to the display, and it should be a Display, not just placement of product as so many are. Rotate different furniture and props in the window so that it looks different with each change.

* Announce the new window to customers, build anticipation for the great reveal!

* Create 4 key windows a year which have extra effort and investment than the regular windows and create events and promotions around them; a gorgeous opulent Christmas window is a good example as opposed to a standard window display.

* Invest in large signage or posters, something that will attract the attention of the pedestrians across the road or drivers in passing cars.

* Make it easy to find the products in the window in the store:
  * Create a special sign or ticket
  * Put them in the same place
  * Ensure staff know where they are so they can easily direct customers
  * Use the items to sell additional products in-store

FLOOR PLAN

The Floor Plan is also part of the store's visual communication. Arrange the store so that traffic is directed to move through/around the store, without the customer realising it, while still making it conducive to shopping.

The 'one-way' traffic Floor Plan works for IKEA. It will not work in most stores, although the idea of moving store traffic in a certain order is a good one. Create a Floor Plan that guides the customer through the store in a way that the products, ideas and uses are 'revealed' to them as they move.

Department and product adjacencies are very important when creating a floor plan. Done properly they will assist sales people when serving customers, provide better customer service and encourage add-on sales.

Relay the store regularly so that it looks fresh as well as show customers products they may have walked past many times before. Remember to keep the fundamentals of the floor plan and make the changes gradually from one to the other so as not to upset regular customers.

DEPARTMENTS

Creating 'Departments' or arranging by product associations, are tools that can be used to ensure the customer shops in comfort while being able to find stock easily and see all the store has to offer. Departments will work only when there is an extensive assortment within the product category.

Good Department adjacencies will encourage add on sales without a staff member's guidance. The customer shopping for a cushion will find table top linens and room candles nearby to be relevant as well as a good suggestion as an add-on for the cushion.

DEPARTMENTS .... cont

The displays near the departments should be used to bring products together and will make add-on sales easier as the customer will see the products in situ, as they would be worn or seen in the home.

VISUAL MERCHANDISING (VM) POINTS

Set up Visual Merchandising (VM) Points throughout the store, inline with the Floor Plan. As the customer moves through the store, they will see different products and combinations to inspire them to buy. This is a great way for a retailer to create impact and show their flair and style that sets them apart from the market.

At each VM Point, create a Vignette (display) that tells a 'story' relevant to the products in their proximity. Continually update and / or totally change the vignette so that regular customers are seeing fresh displays and product. Where possible try to create Vignettes that extend beyond eye level and can be seen from various places in the store.

Incorporate as much product as possible in one Vignette in order to illustrate the scope to the customer and encourage multiple sales.

Vary the heights in the display to make it interesting. Use props to make the Vignette stand out. Use the ceiling where possible and hang items so that the display has movement.

The number and size are dependant on the store. For those who are not creative, be inspired by magazines, suppliers, books or work with an expert.

When product is removed from a Vignette, replace it quickly or redo it, there is nothing worse than a naked mannequin or a 'ravaged' display.

My Visual Communication Notes:

SIGNAGE

Signage is also important to the visual communication with the customer, inside and outside the store.

Outside the store signage must show that the store is there and sets the tone and the customer's expectation. There should be a sign on the awning or the front of the store so that someone across the road can see it AND there should also be a sign at right angles with the store entrance so that foot traffic can see it. This is not an either or, both are a necessity. They should look the same and use the branding design and style. Peeling and fading lettering and signage but be replaced.

The front of the store should not look like a mish-mashed sign collection but must relay some information to customers, when the store is open and closed. The style and design of the Open and Close sign should look like all store signage. Store trading hours should be clearly visible, so too the store phone number, website and any other store locations. Keep this very clean, work with a sign company, they have many options. Frosted stickers are the cleanest and don't interfere with any merchandising or visibility.

I always say that signage should be considered a silent sales person. Signs 'speak' to the customer too – they give information the customer needs to make the buying decision. Do not fill the store with pricing signs, vary the signage size and details, depending on their purpose; in some cases, pricing is appropriate, in others, signage telling the product history, interesting story, award won, interesting fact, additional uses etc are also needed.

Signage style, down to fonts and colours, should be consistent with store branding.

All items in the store should be priced. Ideally each item should be priced but a general sign with pricing and product info for a shelf or table will suffice. Sometimes customers need to know the price before deciding and don't want to ask a sales person. If the item is priced, the sale will not be lost.

SIGNAGE .... cont

Remember, there are customers who don't want to be served by a sales person, they want to shop in their own time and speed and need the information to make the buying decision. This is an extension of good customer service.

NEVER handwrite signs inside or outside the store. ALWAYS print them on a standard office printer or have the 'shell' printed with the logo on top, and add the text and prices with Letraset or invest in alphabetical stamps. The only handwriting that works is calligraphy or a designer's.

Below are some examples of signage styles, where possible, include the store name and or logo for better detail, use links on last page to go online (click the Visual Merchandising QR Codes or link):

QR Codes

I love QR (Quick Response) Codes, which are a specific matrix barcode (or two-dimensional code) that is readable by dedicated QR readers, smartphones, and, to a less common extent, computers with webcams. I use the Optiscan App, on iPhone & iPad, to read them.

They have been designed to allow its contents to be decoded at high speed, which makes them ideal for retail and instant communication.

They encode a URL, text, phone number or sms which are embedded in the square code, like the one on the right.

QR Codes will revolutionise how 'products' share information with customers and how customers access information. By using them in-store, customers will perceive the business as confident with technology and a leader. This will cement their confidence that the store they shop in is on trend and up to date. Use QR Codes on labels and signage where more info or online links are relevant. Put one in the store window that directs the customer to different links; mailing list sign up, special offer, more information, pictures etc. Label the code so they know what to expect.

They are new and they will be used more in the next 12 months in advertising, promotional campaigns and to communicate with customers.

Customers are fast learning that **QR Codes = Action** and they will readily scan them.

Be aware of them and start to incorporate them into the business activity.

STAFF

Staff are an integral part of the store visual communication. How they dress, look, present themselves, speak, interact with the customer as well as each other and ultimately how they sell, all make part of the 'colour' and 'display' inside the store.

Training is vital to ensure the behaviour and experience is consistent throughout the store.

CREATIVE

Creativity cannot be underestimated when creating visual impact. Be clever and funny, not all VM has to be serious, consumers respond well to humour.

Some ideas:

* Use furniture as merchandisers in-store to create a unique ambience, rather than standard shop fittings. This definitely appeals to today's consumer who is looking for familiarity and comfort in their shopping experience.

  Even better would be offering the furniture for sale seasonally so as to refresh the store with new displays and add to the sales in-store.

* Use the stock to create impact, eg: back wall with cushions floor to ceiling or using the same item in different colours or heights, eg: candles

* Use the stock to create a known icon, eg: hats creating the Eiffel Tower or a Ribbon Harbour Bridge.

* Use block colour at Vignettes – bring together many items in the same colour or tone of the colour.

Investing in visual merchandising is important, especially in the current climate. Customers are comparing the store to everything else they see – and they see a LOT! Results will be seen immediately when visual communication is refined.

HOUSEKEEPING

Make Housekeeping a priority: Dust regularly, vacuum daily, keep a tidy and clear counter, clean the store at the end of the day and straighten up at the beginning of the next day.

A messy, dirty store does not encourage customers to enter, not only for basic hygienic reasons but because it says to the customer "We don't really care about our store". Why would they enter?

Boxes on the floor and around the register are a pet hate of mine. They are not only an Occupational Health and Safety issue, they are also messy and affect the 'look' of the store. Boxes should be stored where customers can't see them and only unpacked in quiet times. Stock in boxes can not be sold, boxes should be unpacked within 24 hours of their arrival. This should all be outlined in the Product Procedure (chapter 2).

PRACTICAL EXAMPLE

A Homeware Store.

Within the store there are different departments; candles, candle holders, lamps, frames, cushions, linen, plates & décor, that can be brought together in the Vignettes to create a 'story' and show the different items together as they would be seen in the customer's home.

The Vignettes must relate to each other throughout the store and the front window with the same theme and enhance the products on display.

The Front Window should be a 'big Vignette' and eye catching display that will create impact and entice the customer inside the store. Large posters with blown up graphics set the tone and theme.

The Signage in-store should reflect the colours, the look of the season and the pallet of the homewares in-store – with the overall branding of the business in mind, ie: consistent font and style.

Staff with branded aprons will be protecting their clothes as well as reflecting the feel of the store.

VISUAL COMMUNICATION TAKE AWAY

EVERY single item and intangible element in the store speaks to the customer.

Once the brand, look and feel is determined; it is easy to use this as the style guide for the store's visual communication

VISUAL COMMUNICATION TIPS

* Be guided by the branding and customer in every aspect.

* Create a cohesive floor plan.

* Pay attention to the front window as well as key display points in the store.

* Invest in key props and rotate them throughout the store.

* Ensure lighting is in line with the store ambiance. Use it to attract customers to key areas.

* Create uniform signage that reflects the personality of the store.

* Don't forget the outside of the store.

* Look to large nationally & internationally owned stores for inspiration and adapt it to the store.

* Be Creative and unique with the tools.

We work with clients in all aspects of their branding and visual merchandising. Contact us for more information: info@magnoliasolutions.com.au or phone: +61 2 8003 5585.

EXAMPLES OF WELL EXECUTED VISUAL COMMUNICATION

You can see these pictures in colour online – refer to link to Visual Merchandising on the last page:

A great example of grabbing attention through visual communication; this little girl is mesmerised by the display at **Ted Baker** in Chadstone Shopping Centre, Melbourne

Laduree in Paris, simply use their exquisite instantly recognisable packaging in the window and in store. This is reproduced in all stores all over the world.

EXAMPLES OF WELL EXECUTED VISUAL COMMUNICATION

Marie Papier in Paris, the gorgeous vignettes in-store are an extension of the window display, right.

Marie Papier in Paris, window displays reflect the stylish, elegant signature of the brand.

EXAMPLES OF WELL EXECUTED VISUAL COMMUNICATION

L'Occitane, always have gorgeous front windows. Here, they are appealing to the senses by focusing on the floral impact rather than the product, cream. QVB Sydney

Gorgeous store window in Paris, in the middle of winter, transports the viewer to another place!

EXAMPLES OF WELL EXECUTED VISUAL COMMUNICATION

These 2 pictures are from my favourite front windows of all time! At **Galeries Lafayette** in Paris. (above & below)

Everything in the windows was sprayed the same colour with the paint pots being the only thing untouched. The same window stickers tied all the windows together.

EXAMPLES OF WELL EXECUTED VISUAL COMMUNICATION

Repetition is a great tool to use to create visual impact. Imagine this display with one magazine forward, it would not be as strong.

Thomas Dux using the simple cans of tomatoes to create visual impact – rare good example of handwritten sign.

My Visual Communication To-Do:

My Visual Communication To-Do:

⑦ ONLINE: Website, E-Commerce, Social Media, 'Virtual Store'

This is the last step in creating a great retail business, The first 6 areas must be addressed and developed before moving online. Online activity serves to magnify the offline reality of the business, good and bad, so it's important to eliminate the bad. Think of the online space as a new store location – or five!

The important thing here is to understand the importance of the 'online' space for every retailer and how to use it. The customer is communicating, sourcing and connecting online with the brands, stores and businesses they like. Any business not in this space will miss out.

This is the biggest change in retail ever and requires a serious change of thinking and business activity in order to adapt it into the existing business.

ONLINE

The website is a great opportunity to access customers outside the geographical area of the store. The Global community is getting larger and borders are becoming irrelevant. Retailers can benefit and grow much faster, easier and cheaper than setting up a new store!

Just over a third of Australian retailers have a website. Online sales have increased 10 times more than bricks and mortar retail sales in Australia (the trend is also reflected internationally). Although exact figures are hard to find, over 50% of Online Shopping Sites do not have a bricks and mortar location. This is an opportunity for retailers with a 'real' store that should be used and promoted as such.

Consumers are doing their research and subsequent purchasing online from the comfort of their computer or mobile phone, 24/7. Over 80% of consumers research future purchases online. Consumers are online and on the go, mobile smart phones enable consumers to access the internet whenever they want to, they are no longer bound to a desk.

This technology has enabled the change in consumer behaviour that we see today.

Over 70% of customers who research a purchase online actually buy the product they research. Many customers who research online buy in a bricks and mortar store. Once they know and trust the store after experiencing it, they may order product they know and trust online rather than visit the store for convenience. The point being, they now have options they didn't have before and they are using them!

Retailers can communicate online in a much more personalised way with each customer who can learn about the store and products at their leisure. The customer can choose how and when they shop and retailers know where the customer is and be in the same place!

Although Generation Y and those after them, do not have concerns shopping online, there is still a lot of trepidation from older customers buying online. Having a retail location reinforces that any issues or questions will be answered by a 'real' person. Warranties, security, trust, speed and convenience are all features a bricks and mortar store has that an online store does not have.

The thing I have yet to see done well in Australia is the integration of the website and other online activity in-store. I have been told by retailers that they are 'afraid' to let the customer know they have an online store and presence, in-case they lose them!! This is old thinking and needs to be made extinct!

Customers are in this space. Brands and businesses are communicating with customers.

Customers are connecting with brands and businesses and sharing their activity with their friends (community). Customers are shopping online.

They are there with you or WITHOUT you, so best to be where they are!!

WEBSITE

The website should be the centre of all online activity. All online roads, from Social Media, shopping cart, supplier links etc, lead to the website and the store as well as to each other. This is an illustration of what is should look like, these are by no means the only sites in each category:

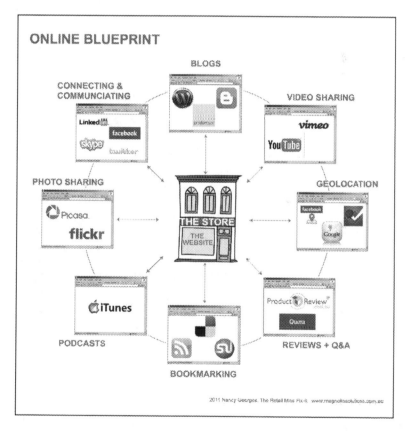

http://www.magnoliasolutions.com.au/book/exclusiv e-access-online-websites-e-commerce-social-media/

WEBSITE .... cont

Every retailer knows the benefit of having 2 stores: Buying stock at better prices, cheaper freight per item, duplicating planning and implementation that happen in one store and easily apply to another store. A website gives the retailer an opportunity operate like they have multiple stores.

Use the customer information and what is known about their spending and product preferences to target them directly with relevant information to let them know about:

* an in-store event
* new product
* clearance of product
* a promotion

This saves unnecessary spending on targeting the wrong customers or in media that do not yield a result. Online, the results and response are immediate and activities can be tweaked and assessed.

The online conversation must be more than clearance sales and selling. Retailers must use the website to build authority and give the customer information. They must have an ongoing conversation.

In the past, especially in Australia, an affordable website was not available. This has now changed with sites such as Wordpress providing a 'free' website for any business. It is not correct to use Social Media pages as a faux website. The website is a business' real estate online and they should own their own space rather than 'rent' it as they with Social Media.

The key word with any website solution that is 'future proof' is **OPEN SOURCE**. Wikipedia defines Open Source as "software for which the original source code is made freely available and may be redistributed with or without modification". This means that as the web rapidly changes the source code is updated at the same speed. It also means the feeds and connections from other online sites, such as Twitter, Facebook, You Tube etc, will feed straight into the site.

WEBSITE .... cont

TIP: Do not work with a programmer who does not work with open source and is not using Social Media in their own business. If they say that Open Source is for Hackers, then you know that they are not equipped to build your online platform and are part of an old system that has not kept up to date.

I built my websites myself using Wordpress with little more than regular computer skills. While not an easy process it allowed me to know what is truly involved and how best to implement this for independent retailers who are under resourced – it can be done!

SEO: Search Engine Optimisation

A great website is useless without 'visitors', a good Search Engine Optimisation (SEO) campaign ensures that the website is found by web browsers and potential customers. Some sites, such as Wordpress, come SEO enabled with blank boxes that have to be filled in. Google is #1 search engine so the focus should be on how to get the site on Google's radar. Google simply want websites with best practices and reward the ones that do.

Some basic SEO Tips:

* use a platform that is inline with current technology – anything open source

* good natural links to & from external sites: Social Media, customers, suppliers, articles etc

* update information regularly

* start a blog and update it regularly

* include pictures and videos

* use Google tools such as Google Places and embed information on the website

TECHNOLOGY

Increasingly, the technology being used is definitely mobile and portable technology. Smart Phones, tablets and e-readers have taken portability beyond the laptop and made it easier to connect than ever before. This must always be a consideration when building new sites and in any new activity: where is the customer viewing the content and how to make it enjoyable for them there.

Tablets are introducing technology to people who had never before used a computer, they are enabling people to read more and browse more. There are over 250 000 Apps (Applications) built for the iPhone and iPad alone. Leverage any Apps that are applicable to the store and promote them to customers.

E-Readers have resulted in 18% more people reading who would never have read a book. This shows the ease of the adoption of the technology.

How can these be used in the business?

E-COMMERCE / SHOPPING CART

For **any** retailer, a website is almost useless without a 'shopping cart' or E-Commerce. The customer expects to be able to purchase on any site they visit. This is the benchmark. Retailers without one are rated poorly by current and potential customers.

Like websites in the past, e-commerce solutions were inaccessible to retailers due to cost. This is no longer the case. There are template solutions that enable the user to fill in preset fields with information. Templates are much cheaper than customised sites which are only relevant for large companies. I recommend starting with a template, after experience and feedback and some sales, then investigate a customised site.

E-COMMERCE / SHOPPING CART .... cont

Considerations when looking at an online 'shopping cart':

* Overall cost: customised vs template.

* Number of products that can be loaded. Is there a limit? Can you upload in bulk?

* Automated shipping and tax calculations.

* Checkout options.

* Supports your Payment Gateway.

* Check out other shopping sites and make a list of what you do & don't like.

* Establish your needs.

* Prioritize your needs based on your list – this is your 'must have' list.

* Mobile versions so that the site can be viewed easily on smart phones and tablets.

* Investigate Templates vs Customised.

Once the online store is set up, it needs to be part of the store's every day activity. When customers shop online, they should be able to pick up the product in the store. Alternatively if they are in the store, they should be able to buy a product and have it delivered to their desired address for the same price as online delivery.

The line between online and offline is disappearing. Customers expect to be able to move from one to the other and interact with the store **where** they choose, **when** they choose.

Having the online shopping facility is not enough, knowing what customers expect from it and how best to use it, is the important thing to learn and master,

E-COMMERCE / SHOPPING CART .... cont

Payment Gateway

Payment Gateways are simply the online 'EFTPOS machine' that processes the payments and takes the money from the customer. They are plugged into the shopping cart and linked to the bank account. I recommend PayPal as a must. Multiple gateways on one site are possible and the customer can choose but having PayPal will ensure the customer is confident they can shop securely which is one of the barriers to online purchasing. This is especially important for international transactions, PayPal is known around the world. Once the customer has had the question of security answered, they will shop freely.

Mobile Technology

Mobile devices are fast emerging as the online shoppers tool of choice. They are **not** just browsing they are connecting, sharing, talking and shopping on their mobile phones. Modern websites have a format for mobile to enable easier browsing on smart phones and tablets. They load faster and are easier to read. Customers will not persist with websites that take too long to load and don't have easy transactions, which makes a mobile format for every website important.

SOCIAL MEDIA

The store should use the website in conjunction with Social Media to build a community of customers and people of **common interest**. It is the common interest that is most important for Social Media and the reason it works. People with the same tastes and preferences will tend to act the same and buy the same things. **Word of Mouth (WOM)** is fast becoming a very important marketing tool. Customers ask friends, colleagues and associates for referrals and suggestions when they are looking to make a purchase, over any other information source, including advertising and sales people.

SOCIAL MEDIA .... cont

By claiming a space in the Social Media landscape a business can leverage the customer's natural activity in Social Media but not try to influence or manipulate it.

It Is important to note that customers are not in Social Media to promote your business!

Social Media enables new and potential customers to be reached, out of the store's geographical area. New Geolocational sites make it even easier to find businesses and share them with friends.

Despite the ease of creating profiles in Social Media and using it, it is very important that it is not the only presence or site the store has online. If the website is the real estate you own, Social Media is the space you rent – there are no guarantees that it will be there tomorrow.

Connecting sites through Autoposting must be done carefully as each site has its own audience and language. Each site is different and people join them for different conversations and reasons, so Autoposting needs to be done carefully.

Social Media is a great research tool and is being used as search engines. Browse for any key word or topic and see what customers are saying about it – then incorporate this into the activity of the store.

It is said that Social Media is a democratiser. It gives users access to people, celebrities and influencers like never before. This makes for a far more interesting and meaningful conversation.

It is very important to be authentic in Social Media, customers will be able to tell quickly and easily if a business is not being authentic and will talk about it online in the public forum – once it is out there it can never be removed.

Whether the business is using all sites or not, reserve the business name on all Social Media sites to ensure it does not get taken by someone else. Try and use the same username / 'handle' across all the sites to make finding the store online easier.

Some common Social Media sites:

Blogs

Blogs are becoming an integral part of any website and in fact many service businesses don't have a separate website, they just have a great blog. The blog should be on the website not in an external site.

The blog is the store's own in-house magazine and should feature all the activity in–store and be interesting. There is a real skill to building and maintaining a blog so make sure the research is done first.

Like the website, content is king in the blog. If the information and content is not relevant, customers will not return. Blogs should be updated regularly and customers updated of the new content.

Facebook

www.facebook.com
www.facebook.com/NancyGeorgesRetailMissFixIt

Facebook is where all the action is at the moment! Social Media moves quickly and there are new sites starting all the time. Facebook is available in over 100 languages which makes it the most attractive platform and the one I suggest every retailer starts with.

Facebook has good business pages, apps and plugins that make the functionality and customer experience a truly interactive one.

Do not create a personal profile page for the business – only a 'Facebook Page', these business pages require a personal profile page in order to be created. Personal profiles require someone to be a 'friend'. Business pages are 'liked'.

Facebook .... cont

Make sure that all the content on Facebook is on the website as well. Continually link to the site and the store and drive customers to both. Run a competition online and give them something if they come into the store. Remember to promote it in-store, online and in customer communication.

Connect and comment on customer activity and invite them to share with their friends. People are comfortable in their Facebook world and will adopt new activity there easier than elsewhere.

People do 3 things in Facebook, they:

1. Comment
2. Like
3. Share

Ensure interesting and relevant information is posted on the page and they will do what they do naturally, by doing any of these 3 things the store or products will then be shared with the customer's community – increasing the online real estate of the store.

Facebook advertising is also a popular tool that businesses use and one that gives good results overall.

I post a **'Tip of the Day'** daily Monday to Friday on the Magnolia Solutions Facebook page: www.facebook.com/NancyGeorgesRetailMissFixIt.

I cover anything and everything in terms of retail, selling, customer service, online, social media, business etc. Please let me know if you have any suggestions or questions!

My Social Media Notes:

Twitter

www.twitter.com   www.twitter.com/NancyGeorges

Twitter is not just a micro-blogging site. It is a true connecting site where people of similar interests share info and news faster than any other platform in the world. The comment is often made that people check Twitter for the news first rather than radio or TV. Twitter certainly comes with better commentary than the news! Twitter activity is fast and furious and it has a language all of its own. Make the time to learn and observe the rules of Twitter before plunging in.

The speed of Twitter means that the Social Media strategy must take into account that a large majority of the community may miss the conversation. Be repetitive but don't cut and past, be creative and clever.

A great example of Twitter used well by a store, is the baker who tweets out that the fresh sourdough rolls will be out of the oven at 1.00pm and sells out of them as people have queued for the fresh stock, which sells out in 30 minutes.

Another clever use of Twitter is to announce a 'Spot Special' for a limited time, ideally this would be a quiet time or when there is something to clear,

Photo Sharing Sites

This was the first thing that people did with the emergence of social media. How great was it being able to see overseas friends' pictures as they happen? Creating albums, editing them, adding pictures are all things that customers expect to be able to do with photos online.

Facebook took this even further with tagging people for easy sorting and increasing interaction.

Other common photo sharing sites are **Flickr** and **Picasa**.

Again, it is important to be in the appropriate sites so as to get on the customer's radar. Good use of these sites for stores is to feature the store, pics, products, staff and customers in different albums. Don't forget to update the same information on the website and to point all activity on these sites to the store and to the website.

You Tube

www.youtube.com   www.youtube.com/MagnoliaSolutions

Remember a picture tells a thousand words and talking pictures are even more effective!

You Tube is the number 2 search engine in the world. Customers are searching in it and the store must have a presence so as not to miss out. Making videos is no longer difficult, but they must reflect the store's branding and not be too amateurish.

Create a channel for the store and post videos showing the activity in store, products, staffs and customers. How great is that?? Who needs a TV station when you can be your own Steven Spielberg!!

Every video uploaded to You Tube will have its own embed code which makes it look very professional when it is embedded on the website. Sharing and tracking videos have never been easier! The information and data can be used to further connect with the customers and the areas the video is most played and shared in. **Always** embed the videos on the website, don't just upload them all on You Tube.

Bookmarking Sites

There is a lot of information on the web and Bookmarking Sites have emerged to solve the problem of how to sort and read favourite sites and new information that is relevant to the browser. The concept is easy and works exactly the same way that a bookmark works in a book – making it easy to find later. New information is key here. If new information is not regularly added the website will not appear on the bookmarking sites.

Once a user tags a site they like on a bookmarking site, they nominate how often they would like to receive notifications of updates or they log onto the site and see the information in one place. It is like creating a personalised daily magazine with only the things the user likes.

RSS (Really Simple Syndication) feeds enable the sites to be bookmarked, they flag updated content and are then grabbed by the bookmarking sites.

Bookmarking sites include: **Delicious, StumbleUpon, Digg, Reddit, Google Reader** but there are many more.

Social Bookmarking is also emerging, bookmarking is more valuable when it is shared. Sites such as **Polyvore** and **Pinterest** are popular and easy to use.

My Social Media Notes:

Google

www.google.com

Google is the number 1 search engine in the world. They have moved beyond only being a search engine and are now incorporating:

* email
* calendar
* business tools - including Google Alerts & Google Places
* maps
* video - You Tube
* images
* geolocational tools – including Google Earth
* web analytics – Google Analytics
* internet browser - Firefox
* targeted advertising
* translator
* iGoogle – creating a personalised home page
* Google Reader – bookmarking tool
* IMTalk

These tools are not only useful and will add value to the business but also the more Google features used, will help with SEO.

The most important Google tool for any retailer with a physical location is the free **Google Places** which works in conjunction with Google Maps. When a customer searches a location, street or suburb, the Google Places post shows up in the search. Stores with a Google Places pages appear towards the top of the search results and are far more prominent than other text-only listings. It has been proven to convert a view into a click vs other businesses without a Google Place post.

Google .... cont

Google Places doesn't replace a website but extends the 'online real estate' of the store, as well as provides space for the store to provide detailed information, web links, post pictures, publish opening hours, points of difference etc.

Geolocational Sites

Geolocational sites match the users preference with products and services nearby. This activity can then be shared across social media sites, making it interactive for the user and their friends as well as the business.

These sites are accessed primarily through smart phones as they require the user to 'check-in' to a physical location. Users love using them and freely share their location, comments and pictures on the sites and subsequently with their friends.

For this reason, it is important that every retailer be on these sites. If users don't find the store on the site, they can create the post themselves, invariably this will have little or no information. It is not always possible to change incorrect information. Every retailer must claim their page on these sites and fill it with as much information as is possible. The next step is to show and tell your customers that the store is on the sites and encourage them to check in, while in the store – what a great way to promote the store!

Retailers can now see who has been in their store, where they were before and where they go after being in their business **in real time**. It is this immediacy that is as valuable as the information itself.

Offers should always be made to regular customers as well as to entice new customers to the store, but they must check-in to be eligible, ie: physically be in the store.

Food sellers seem to be the retailers that get this consistently correct. They offer a size upgrade, additional muffin, 5th coffee free etc to those who check in at certain times.

Geolocational Sites .... cont

Popular sites are:

Four Square   www.foursquare.com

  Retailers must claim the Google Places location first in order to claim the Four Square location. These stickers can be placed in-store, online and on any other promotional activity to promote the store.

The customer who checks in the most in 60 days becomes the mayor of the store. Badges, points and rewards are given to users for different types of check-ins, so there is a game element.

Facebook Places

Although the application is not as developed as Four Square, users find it easy to check in using a site they are comfortable with and they can tag friends who are with them which will show on both of their pages.

ANAYLSE

Analyse every single online activity, replicate and expand on what worked and stop what is not working. The data can be taken from the analytic tools on the website, Social Media measurements and Google Analytics which can be linked to the site.

This information will show where customers were before they came to the site, the keywords they used to find the site, what other businesses they like as well as where they go when they leave the site. This is a great insight into the customer behaviour and an effective accurate way to find collaborators and competitors.

PRACTICAL EXAMPLE

Retailer:

bricks-n-mortar store with website, social media and online store.

Event:
In-store event with special offer to VIP customers.

Activity:

- promote event in-store with signage, to increase awareness as well as to encourage customers who have not signed to the store mailing list to sign up

- promote event and special VIP offer to the mailing list through email newsletter

- promote event on the website to increase awareness as well as to encourage customers who have not signed to the store mailing list to sign up, it should appear:
    - somewhere on the home page
    - on the events page
    - on the VIP customer page
    - on the contact us page
    - as a blog post promoting the event details and the benefits of attending and any photos of past events

- promote the event on social media pages to increase awareness as well as to encourage customers who have not signed to the store mailing list to sign up, link all posts to the mailing list signup page as well as the blog

- the blog should be automatically linked to at least the Facebook page, the Facebook page should be linked to twitter so the message will duplicate itself (Autoposting)

- announce the event with at least a month's notice – then closer to the time more frequently – but change the information and content so the customer doesn't feel bombarded or 'spammed' with the same message

PRACTICAL EXAMPLE .... cont

- **During the event**:

  - take lots of pictures and regularly post status updates and some picture.

  - Ask customers to give quotes and comments and post them.

  - Encourage everybody to 'checkin' and claim an offer

- **After the event**:

  - Write a blog post and add all pics, info and feedback

  - Send a newsletter to the entire database and thank customers who attended, show some of the prizes, gifts or offers and link to blog post

  - Put link to blog on social media sites

  - Upload photos to online sharing

Inform and educate staff about the information posted as well as the results so they encourage customers to join in the activity.

My Social Media Notes:

ONLINE TAKE AWAY

EVERY retailer must be online, have an online store and use social media across every platform. It is not enough to have these tools, they must be used properly and together.

ONLINE TIPS

* Make sure the store and the business itself is as good as it can be and that the first 6 steps, as above, have been addressed.

* Create an overall plan and strategy for all online activity before starting.

* Start with a website based on an open source platform and work with programmers and suppliers who understand and use open source and social media in their own businesses.

* Find a shopping cart that will fit with the website and meet the needs of the business.

* Sign up to as many social media sites as are relevant to the store even if they are not going to be used initially, so that the name is taken by the store.

* Create pages on all geolocational sites and Google Places.

* Fill out as much information about the store on all pages, sites and applications that all lead to the store as well as the website.

* Remember: Content is King so make information interesting and relevant to the customer.

* Inform and train staff so they incorporate it in their conversation with customers.

We work with clients to develop their online presence that is inline with their offline reality. Nancy is available to speak at conferences, exhibitions & association events on this topic as well as those covered in this book.
Contact us for more information: info@magnoliasolutions.com.au
or phone: +61 2 8003 5585.

My Online To Do:

My Online To Do:

Thank You

Thank you for taking the time to read this book. I hope you have pages of notes and ideas that you will implement in your retail business! As retailers, it is up to all of us to ensure that independent retail not only survives but thrives and grows!

I will be releasing more books focused on retail and will be launching a low priced, easy to manage website and shopping cart product that will enable moving online to happen quickly and easily using modern, up to date platforms, tools and support. Please make sure you are signed up for my News and Updates via the link on the website.

If you need further help in your business, with one on one consulting or a 4 Hour Power Meeting, would like to attend Retail Marketing Seminars, would like me to speak at your conference, exhibition or event or anything else, please contact me.

Happy Sales & Connecting!

Cheers

Nancy

Connect with

Nancy Georges
The Retail Miss Fix It

Web :	www.magnoliasolutions.com.au
Blog :	www.magnoliasolutions.com.au/blog
Twitter:	www.twitter.com/NancyGeorges
Facebook:	www.facebook.com/NancyGeorgesRetailMissFixIt
LinkedIn:	www.linkcdin.com/in/nancygeorges
Posterous:	www.nancygeorges.posterous.com
YouTube:	www.youtube.com/MagnoliaSolutions
Things I Like:	www.pinterest.com/Nancy_Georges/
Instagram:	NancySnapper
Email:	info@magnoliasolutions.com.au
Phone Number:	+61 2 8003 5585

Or scan here to go to the Contact Us page online and click away!

7 Powerful Ways to Boost Retail Profits
....in any economic climate
The New Rules
A successful, profitable business requires skill, planning & strategy

CONNECT ONLINE

Scan the QR Codes and be taken to Exclusive Access Pages for each Topic, or type the links on the next page straight into your address bar:

7 Powerful Ways to Boost Retail Profits
....in any economic climate
The New Rules
A successful, profitable business requires skill, planning & strategy

CONNECT ONLINE

Type the links below straight into your address bar and be taken to Exclusive Access Pages for each Topic:

1.   Marketing
http://www.magnoliasolutions.com.au/book/exclusive-access-marketing/

2.   Systems, Procedures & Policies
http://www.magnoliasolutions.com.au/book/exclusive-access-systems-procedures-policies/

3.   Staff Training & Leadership
http://www.magnoliasolutions.com.au/book/exclusive-access-staff-training-leadership/

4.   Customers & Customer Service
http://www.magnoliasolutions.com.au/book/exclusive-access-customers-customer-service/

5.   Products
http://www.magnoliasolutions.com.au/book/exclusive-access-products/

6.   Visual Communication
http://www.magnoliasolutions.com.au/book/exclusive-access-visual-merchandising/

7.   Online: Websites, E-Commerce, Social Media
http://www.magnoliasolutions.com.au/book/exclusive-access-online-websites-e-commerce-social-media/